Lincoln's Notebooks

Lincoln's Notebooks

Letters, Speeches, Journals, and Poems

Edited by

DAN TUCKER

Introduction by Harold Holzer

BLACK DOG
& LEVENTHAL
PUBLISHERS
NEW YORK

Black Dog & Leventhal Publishers
Hachette Book Group
1290 Avenue of the Americas
New York, NY 10104
www.hachettebookgroup.com
www.blackdogandleventhal.com

First Edition: August 2017

Black Dog & Leventhal Publishers is an imprint of Hachette Books, a division of Hachette Book Group.
The Black Dog & Leventhal Publishers name and logo are trademarks of Hachette Book Group, Inc.
The publisher is not responsible for websites (or their content) that are not owned by the publisher.
The Hachette Speakers Bureau provides a wide range of authors for speaking events.
To find out more, go to www.HachetteSpeakersBureau.com or call (866) 376-6591.

Print book interior design by Liz Driesbach

Library of Congress Cataloging-in-Publication Data has been applied for.

ISBNs: 978-0-316-38989-1 (hardcover); 978-0-316-31949-2 (ebook)

Printed in China

1010

10 9 8 7 6 5 4 3 2 1

CONTENTS

~

This portrait of Lincoln from February 1861 by Springfield photographer Christopher German is the last one made before Lincoln left Illinois for Washington to assume the presidency.

INTRODUCTION
At a Loss for Words by Harold Holzer

Writing of the thunderbolt 1862 announcement of Abraham Lincoln's greatest act, the Emancipation Proclamation, in his *History of the English-Speaking Peoples*, Winston Churchill made a keen observation:

> In Britain it was not understood why [Lincoln] had not declared Abolition outright. A political maneuver on his part was suspected. . . . In America . . . the Democratic Party in the North was wholly opposed. . . . In the Federal armies it was unpopular. . . . At the Congressional elections in the autumn of 1862 the Republicans lost ground. Many Northerners thought that the President had gone too far, others that he had not gone far enough. Great, judicious, and well-considered steps are thus sometimes at first received with public incomprehension.[1]

Churchill's points were well taken. At the time it was issued, Lincoln's proclamation left both ardent antislavery and rigidly proslavery advocates dissatisfied—abolitionists because it failed to free slaves everywhere, slaveowners because it freed them anywhere. For good measure, its announcement also agitated Union loyalists in slave-holding border states, exempted from the order but sensitive now to the inevitability of freedom. The edict managed as well to outrage countless Federal soldiers who believed they had enlisted in the army solely to preserve the government, not to free slaves. And the proclamation vexed anti-Abolitionist, pro-Democratic Party Union generals, along with whites in the Confederacy, and for good measure the British press, which feared it would ignite a "servile war" that would cause "blood" " and "shrieks" to come "piercing through the darkness." Amidst such a calamity, the *London Times* hysterically predicted, Lincoln "will rub his hands and think that revenge is sweet."[2]

Lincoln's response to all the criticism? Not a word. It is worth noting—although Churchill, perhaps out of kindness, did not—that the failure of the American public to rally immediately 'round Lincoln's greatest act may have been attributable at least in part to something very un-Churchillian, and for that matter un-Lincolnian as well: public silence. In fact, while most modern Americans justly regard his words as canonical, Lincoln remained similarly silent for most of his embattled presidency. His administration was more often characterized by the absence of words than by oratory. Understanding that largely forgotten historical reality makes this collection all the more precious, for it documents in a lively and accessible manner the ways Lincoln tested his creative gifts to communicate forcefully to the American public during the Civil War: through the power and publication of his writing, even if tradition required that his voice be stilled.

To be sure, Lincoln wrote to be heard by live audiences for most of his three-decade-long public career. Appropriately, this volume abounds with examples, though many originals do not survive in his own hand. (Lincoln did not bother to have his texts archived until he began employing private secretaries in 1860; until then, seeing his speeches in newspaper print was all that mattered to him.) Nonetheless, his surviving jottings and drafts, in increasingly neat penmanship over the years (quite the opposite of the indecipherable chicken-scratches over which researchers labor today) reveal a keen mind and a sure hand. On the following pages, we can almost imagine ourselves back in the nineteenth century, eavesdropping on Lincoln as his thoughts spilled over into words. He composed more than a million in all, though the highlights presented here will prove more than sufficient to testify to his creative genius and hard labor.

The influential stem-winders of the 1850s are of course still worth remembering: his long oration at Peoria, all but introducing the new anti-slavery Republican Party (page 50); his passionate attack on the Supreme Court's Dred Scott decision; and the amusing, if choppy speeches and rejoinders at his 1858 U.S. Senate debates with Stephen Douglas (page 72)—although, as they say, you had to be there. However lacerating his quick wit on the stump, Lincoln was never a great extemporaneous speaker, and the debates, famous as they have become in American political lore, brought out the best in neither the Republican nor Democratic candidates. Ingeniously, Lincoln made certain the flawed results would be remembered in spite of themselves, and would serve as a kind of personal platform two years later when he sought the presidency—because by that time tradition forbade him from saying more. Ironically, the collection of debate transcripts—edited and engineered by Lincoln himself—became a bestseller just as their "author" went publicly mute. With rare exceptions, we sometimes forget, he remained so for the rest of his life, including his years in the White House. Thus the explanatory rhetoric he withheld from the Emancipation Proclamation was a rule, not an exception.

What makes Lincoln's presidential communication particularly fascinating—and riveting examples abound in this collection—is that he wrote so much in the White House yet said so little. He had finally assumed a position of leadership from which to unleash his astonishing vocabulary and arresting style nationwide. But because the "bully pulpit" did not yet exist, the words he did issue remained largely unspoken. Chief executives of the day were expected to refrain from addressing their constituents publicly. Accordingly, Lincoln held no signing ceremony, gave no interviews, issued no additional statements, and made no speeches to explain, amplify, or herald the freedom document he knew would not only outrage some Americans and alter the rationale for the entire Civil War, but also make his name long endure in the annals of humankind. He merely ordered the Emancipation Proclamation published, and allowed its dry, legalistic prose to carry the weight of its history-altering message. To a voluble leader like Churchill, accustomed to leading with words—on the streets, at the House of Parliament, on the radio—it must have been hard to understand, much less explain, how Lincoln's most momentous decision had arrived on the American scene in almost stealthy silence. But sometimes the truth runs against the grain of myth.

In Europe, another master of communications who lived in the Lincoln era, Karl Marx, was similarly shocked when Lincoln's document became public. Marx complained that it lacked ornate eloquence: Lincoln

> always presents the most important act in the most insignificant form possible. Others, when dealing with square feet of land, proclaim it a 'struggle for ideas.' Lincoln, even when he is dealing with *ideas,* proclaims their 'square feet.' Hesitant, resistant, unwilling, he sings the bravura aria of his role as though he begged pardon for the circumstances that forced him 'to be a lion.' . . . His most recent proclamation—the Emancipation Proclamation—the most significant document in American history since the founding of the Union, and one which tears up the old American Constitution, bears the same character.[3]

Unavoidably, the only 1862 statement by Lincoln on Emancipation that Winston Churchill could quote in his great *History* was an excerpt from a now-famous letter Lincoln had written to New York newspaper publisher Horace Greeley precisely a month before issuing the preliminary proclamation: "My paramount object," Lincoln had insisted, "is to save the Union, and is not either to save or destroy slavery. . . . What I do about slavery and the coloured race, I do because it helps to save the Union and what I forbear, I forbear because I do *not* believe it would help to save the Union" (page 139). While the words were designed to prepare a dubious public for a controversial policy change, some interpreters since have argued that they reveal Lincoln as a calculating politician, not a genuine liberator. Such assessments miss the entire point of Lincoln's presidential writing—its uncanny success at changing hearts and minds through logic, not passion, and through powerful words alone, not personal appearances.

Interestingly, these, the most revealing sentences Lincoln ever wrote about Emancipation—as often misunderstood today as they are quoted—were more than anything else, deceptive, revealing another side of Lincoln the writer: not informing, but *mis*informing the public. A few days earlier, Greeley had published a stinging rebuke of the Lincoln Administration, charging that the president had been "strangely and disastrously remiss" for failing, after more than a year of war, to do anything to destroy the institution that had caused it—human slavery.[4] Lincoln's response was not out of character—either in tone or form. Rhetorically, it was classic Lincoln: what I *do*, I do to *achieve* my goal; what I *don't* do, I don't do to achieve the *same* goal; if I could succeed by doing *nothing*, I would do it; if I could succeed by doing *something*, I would do *that*. And then the famous, humanizing caveat: this constituted "no modification of my oft-expressed personal wish that all men every where could be free."

No wonder Greeley threw up his hands in exasperation when he read the letter—especially after Lincoln made certain it was first published in rival papers throughout the country (to get Greeley's goat). Outmaneuvered, the editor sputtered: "I have no doubt that Lincoln's letter had been prepared before he ever saw my 'Prayer,' and that this was merely used by him as an opportunity, an occasion, an excuse for setting his own altered opinion—changed not by his volition, but by circumstances—fairly before the country."[5] Only later, and not for publication, did Greeley admit that the ingenious president made "me appear as an officious meddler in affairs that properly belong to the government. No, I can't trust your 'honest Old Abe," Greeley admitted. "He is too smart for me!"[6]

Greeley was onto something crucial. Lincoln's letter adroitly reinforced his consistent message that his government would address the issue only to save the Union, not necessarily to free the slaves. As Lincoln well knew when he wrote that letter, he had already determined to do just what he had told Greeley he had not yet decided on! The proclamation was already drafted. On the advice of his Cabinet, the cunning president was merely waiting for a battlefield victory so the document could be issued on a wave of success—not as what one minister feared would otherwise be seen as a "last *shriek*, on the retreat."[7]

Lincoln may have had it both ways in 1862, but the judgment of history has been harsher. For generations, his critics (along with a number of ill-motivated white supremacists) have cited the Greeley letter as evidence that Lincoln did not really care about slaves at all. True, Lincoln might have done his reputation (not to mention the resulting political crisis) more good by speaking out publicly. But there would be no further words from Lincoln that year, certainly not from his own lips, in public, to amplify the proclamation that ultimately transformed him, in the estimate of many contemporaries, into the Great Emancipator. And the positive reception enjoyed by the Greeley letter emboldened Lincoln to adapt this means of communication in the future—the creation of ostensibly personal letters and responses written to be read by every American.

Appropriately, this book features not only Lincoln's draft of the epochal Emancipation Proclamation, but also Lincoln's handwritten letter to Greeley, showing—through cross-outs, revisions, pasted-in emendations, and his firm, free handwriting—how his precise mind worked, and how he struggled to overcome the traditional lock imposed on his public communication. Of course it should be acknowledged that, in the short term, the Greeley strategy failed. A few weeks after the Emancipation went public, as Churchill briefly noted, voters in the North dealt Lincoln's Republicans a major blow in off-year Congressional elections. The party lost several governorships and state legislatures, including the assembly and senate in Lincoln's own Illinois. Sometimes the power of even masterful words can do no better than stave off total disaster—they take time to enter the realm of classic political literature. The reader might want to ponder whether the Union could have survived beyond 1862 had Lincoln not insisted in his Greeley message that his emancipation goals were military, rather than philanthropic. And readers of this book must always keep in mind that not everything Lincoln said or wrote during his lifetime won universal acclaim.

To best understand and appreciate this extraordinary treasury, the Greeley letter should be viewed as quintessential Lincoln, not only in tone but also in form and format. It originated as a handwritten document: not as a publicly delivered speech, but as what came to be called a "public letter" and published nationwide. It is hard to imagine, but the leader who had earned his spectacular political reputation as a frontier debater, who had thrilled audiences in Indiana, Ohio, Kansas, and New York City in the months leading up to his nomination, became largely mute. The orator who had offered exhausting stem-winding speeches that enthralled, entertained, and engaged with a new kind of political idiom—less bombast, more humor, more legalistic parrying—had become, as candidate and president-elect, to paraphrase the Greeley criticism that provoked his famous response, "strangely and sometimes disastrously" uncommunicative. Not, as this book shows, with his pen. Although constrained by tradition from orating in public, he nevertheless went on to craft a series of letters on issues ranging from civil liberties to black enlistment that, duplicating the Greeley model, he published in the press without articulating them in person.

Lincoln evinced this steely, almost stubborn, resistance to public speaking from the moment he became the Republican candidate for president in May 1860. His principal opponent, Stephen Douglas, did appear before the public after becoming the Northern Democratic nominee (albeit on the pretext of needing a long train trip to see his ailing mother in Vermont—a trip conveniently interrupted at every railroad station from Illinois east for a speaking opportunity). But Lincoln stayed home in Springfield and steadfastly refused to add anything new to his canon of broadly published, widely distributed earlier speeches. When he visited his own mother that fall, he offered well-wishers only a "hearty greeting," insisting the time to talk policy "had not come." Then he shook hands all around and left to "hearty cheering."

By then, significantly, he had personally seen to the printing of the texts of the famous Lincoln–Douglas debates, and had hand-edited a final version of his 1860 New York Cooper Union speech—which circulated in pamphlet form in New York, Washington, Detroit, Chicago, and other cities. Now he chose silence—declining to say or write anything new, as he put it, cautiously marking his few policy letters "confidential" and "strictly private."[8]

"I could say nothing which I have not already said, and which is in print, open to inspection of all," he explained to a nervous Connecticut official in late 1860. "To press a repetition of this upon those who have listened, is useless; to press it upon those who have *refused* to listen, and *still* refuse, would be wanting in self-respect, and . . . have an appearance of sycophancy and timidity, which would excite the contempt of *good* men, and encourage *bad* ones to clamor the more loudly." The famous debater would debate no more. "I am not at liberty to shift my ground," he told a critic a few days later—"that is out of the question." New speeches, he reiterated, would not only do no good, but "do positive harm."[9]

As we know, South Carolina greeted Lincoln's election with an ordinance of secession, in the wake of which Lincoln steadfastly maintained his "masterly inactivity" and public silence. Other states followed out of the Union before he ever left for Washington, but still the president-elect said nothing. He did offer an emotional farewell to his neighbors in Springfield on February 11, 1861, but in those remarks, he said little to reassure the frightened public—only to convey his reliance on God to guide him through a task, he had no doubt, would be "greater than that which rested upon Washington" (page 98)—in itself an astonishing claim at a time when people on both sides of the Mason–Dixon Line regarded George Washington as an incomparable demigod. Though spoken aloud, without a text, at a railroad station, Lincoln's farewell address offers another impressive example of his skills as a writer and editor. Lincoln had assured newspapermen on the scene that he would say nothing at all before his train departed his hometown. Moments later, overcome by emotion, he launched into his brief but elegiac goodbye. Once the engine lurched forward, correspondents who had missed the newsworthy talk begged the president-elect to supply his text. But Lincoln had none. Instead he obligingly commenced writing, then dictating, then again writing a polished version of the impromptu thoughts he had just offered. A comparison between the version transcribed by a Springfield stenographer at the depot and the revision penciled on the rocky train bound for Washington reveals a brilliant craftsman at work refining his thoughts. Here we get a rare glimpse at a brilliant thought leader in the very process of preparing a message for the public on tight deadline.

In the days that followed on the road, Lincoln at first seemed content only to exchange pleasantries and offer jokes, or to assure state legislatures that he was but a modest man who happened to be ascending to the highest office in his country, and could do little harm before a new man came along four years hence. In all, he repeated his non-message more than a hundred times along his zig-zagging route to the capital.

Only when his inaugural procession reached the East did he seem, almost magically, to come to the realization that something more was expected of him. Ultimately, he rose to the challenge with a stirring speech in Trenton in which he finally confided, recalling the founding fathers: "I am exceedingly anxious that that thing which they struggled for; that something even more than National Independence; that something that held out a great promise to all the people of the world to all time to come . . . shall be perpetuated in accordance with the original idea for which that struggle was made." The next morning, he stunned an audience outside Independence Hall, by declaring, his voice choking with emotion, "I would rather be assassinated on this spot than to surrender it."[10] He never let on that assassination was vividly on his mind that day, having just been warned that a credible death threat awaited him on the final leg of his inaugural journey through Baltimore. Some things could be shared with the public—others, not.

Had Lincoln not sullied this new oratorical momentum by choosing to abide by his advisors' fears and slipping through Baltimore to evade the suspected assassination plot—in some semblance of disguise—his inaugural journey might have been heralded as one of the most successful in history. Baltimore notwithstanding, it was precisely that: a brilliant balancing act incorporating homespun stories designed to stimulate public affection, and literate, passionate references to the Constitution and the founders to build public confidence. In the bargain, Lincoln deftly claimed the icons of history for the cause of Union—even though most of them had been born in the South.

Still, once sworn in, and with a monumental and long underappreciated first inaugural address behind him—another effort reflecting his skill at editing, not just writing (page 106) —Lincoln grew more Whiggish than ever when it came to presidential oratory. He seemed to believe the letter of tradition: that presidents were chosen by electors, not by direct vote of the people, and thus were not supposed to appeal to citizens on a regular basis. His office hours were generous and exhausting; even in the crucible of war, he welcomed strangers to the White House on the most routine business.[11] But communicate with them directly, and en masse? No more.

It is hard to imagine, but once installed at the House, Lincoln all but disappeared from view—except for a few flag-raisings and troop reviews. The United States does not require its chief executives to come before its legislative branch to report and defend their policies. The president is not by, of, and for the Congress, as the prime minister is in Great Britain. Since the John Adams administration, no president had even given his annual messages to Congress—the nineteenth-century versions of today's State of the Union messages—in person. True to tradition, Lincoln sent all five of his own messages—one special and four annual—to Capitol Hill each year via a White House secretary. There, they were read aloud by a clerk of the House. "We cannot escape history," he said memorably in the 1862 iteration. "The fiery trial through which we pass, will light us down in honor or dishonor, to the latest generation." How moving that might have sounded had Lincoln delivered those words himself—but he did not. A functionary read them aloud, maybe without expression; the public read them the next day in the press.

Lincoln's presidential mailbag overflowed with invitations to events that no modern president would think of ignoring: to rallies; meetings; a ceremony to celebrate the transcontinental railroad; innumerable events with his troops (only a handful of which Lincoln graced with his presence); the chance to return to Cooper Union, the scene of one of his greatest triumphs; and to return home to Springfield for a mass rally of loyal Union men who sorely needed a dressing-down about their racist resistance to black resistance. They all elicited refusals: opportunities offered, declined, and lost. "If I were as I have been for most of my life," Lincoln awkwardly told a group of well-wishers who gathered to see him during an impromptu visit to Frederick, Maryland, "I might perhaps talk amusing to you for half an hour, and it wouldn't hurt anybody." But now, he explained, "it is hardly proper for me to make speeches. Every word is so closely noted that it will not do to make trivial ones, and I cannot be expected to make a matured one just now." What he had said on the eve of his presidency still applied: "I am rather inclined to silence."[12]

"In my present position," he told a supporter who had urged him to speak at a Union Mass Meeting in Buffalo timed to occur during the 1864 presidential election campaign: "I believe it is not customary for one holding the office, and being a candidate for re-election, to do so." As always, he preferred a "public letter," and produced one that could be read aloud by someone else. It proved a stirring defense of his administration's refusal to acquiesce in public calls for an armistice that might save lives, but would spell the destruction of the Union. And it ended with a ringing reiteration of the president's faith in newly recruited African American troops.[13]

By then, Abraham Lincoln, still consummately famous as an orator, had perfected the art of the written public message—through which he could, in a way, remain heard but not seen. There was the 1864 letter to Buffalo; a long, tough, well-received 1863 letter to Albany Democrats who had questioned his broad use of executive powers to suppress the rebellion (page 171); and his rather ugly August 1862 comments to a deputation of free African Americans—calling bluntly for their banishment and colonization—crafted to be read in the press by whites to remind them that their president harbored no philanthropic desire to give comfort to people of color (page 137). Such expressions of sympathy might have driven the border states into the Confederacy, dooming the struggle to hold the fragile Union coalition together.

Most famous of all, perhaps, was Lincoln's extraordinary open letter to the citizens of his home town—perhaps his greatest undelivered "speech" (page 179).

In response to this one enticing occasion, Lincoln vacillated. The exchange of letters with his host, onetime neighbor James C. Conkling, indicates that he did, in fact, want very much to return to Springfield to speak for himself, tradition be damned. "I think I will go," he hinted a week before the event—"or send a letter," adding, almost schizophrenically, "—probably the latter."[14] His inevitable final "note" explained: "It would be very agreeable to me to . . . meet my old friends at my own home, but I cannot just now be absent from here, so long as a visit there would require." Instead he asked Conkling to pronounce it aloud—with one suggestion that offers a priceless hint at his own style of public speaking: "Read it very slowly."[15]

"You say you will not fight to free negroes," he bluntly told his neighbors in that text. "Some of them seem willing to fight for you. . . . And then, there will be some black men who can remember that, with silent tongue, and clenched teeth, and steady eye, and well-poised bayonet, they have helped mankind on to this great consummation; while, I fear, there will be some white ones, unable to forget that, with malignant heart, and with deceitful speech, they have strove to hinder it." To be sure, these were dazzling words—and widely published—but like so many of Lincoln's greatest as president, unspoken by the great orator who wrote them to be said aloud. Worse, when the earliest press reprints appeared annoyingly garbled, Lincoln may have resolved that his next invitation to make a speech—at Gettysburg, as it transpired—would not be declined. Lincoln would not only agree to help dedicate the Soldiers' National Cemetery on that hallowed battlefield on November 19, 1863, he would examine and correct the Associated Press transcription before departing.[16]

In considering Lincoln's presidential writing—or a book that showcases that writing—it is thus crucial to keep in mind what a rare and reluctant public speaker he became. He delivered two inaugural addresses—each in its own way a masterpiece. He spoke haltingly, and unmemorably, at a charity fair in Philadelphia late in the war, and once unexpectedly addressed a crowd at a New Jersey train station with all the grace of a deer in the headlights when caught returning to Washington after what he had thought was a top-secret strategy meeting with retired General Winfield Scott. "The Secretary of War, you know, holds a pretty tight rein on the Press," he tried joking that day, "and I'm afraid that if I blab too much he might draw a tight rein on me." As president, the master public speaker did not "blab too much."[17] He pursued a policy of speaking as seldom as possible.

The presidency ironically silenced Abraham Lincoln. His pen was still as mighty as the sword; but his once powerful voice disappeared. His reticence makes his written oeuvre all the more intriguing, all the more worthy of study, and all the more extraordinary, especially when his writing provides up-close and personal glimpses of his creative technique, however muzzled. Some of Lincoln's most memorable words reached only a few people—his confidential letters to reluctant generals, grieving widows and orphans, or his own high-strung wife. Many, in their own way, count as masterpieces, too.

When one thinks about the majesty, power, and durability of Lincoln's apogee—the Gettysburg Address (page 185)—it is not unreasonable to suggest that its reputation owes at least something not just to its literary qualities, but to the shock value that came when the president of the United States actually appeared in person and delivered, if not a full-throated oration as in his pre-presidential days, at least what his hosts called "a few appropriate remarks."[18] These words would cement his reputation as one of the great orators of history, and took days of careful attention to create. Yet many Americans have been convinced since the time of its delivery that Lincoln dashed off those words in haste, perhaps even onboard the train carrying him to Gettysburg the day before. Nothing could be further from the truth—as if the blurred scrawl of his 1861 farewell address was not enough to convince the modern reader that Lincoln did not enjoy writing while riding on the "cars." As the drafts reproduced in this book make clear—from the first to the last of the five copies he wrote before and after the Gettysburg ceremony—Lincoln labored diligently on this, as he did on his other masterworks, crafting and recrafting his immaculate sentences until they sparkled like gems. Few books have made a more sincere effort to record his creative process. Among many critical comments, pro and con, mostly divided along party lines, the *Springfield Republican* was all but alone in recognizing "strong feelings and a large brain were its parents—a little painstaking, its *accoucheur*."[19]

The assassination that stilled his voice—and his pen—so prematurely came just 17 months after his appearance at Gettysburg, and only six weeks after taking the oath of office for a second time by urging a war-weary nation to pursue peace "with malice toward none" (page 208). His death deprived the country of what one contemporary called a "guiding hand, which alone could have solved the problems of reconstruction and added to the triumph of armies those lasting victories which are gained over the hearts of men." A few days before his murder, Lincoln appeared before his public from a White House window to speak "not in sorrow, but in gladness of heart" about the future of his tired country. It was a long speech, and not a very memorable one, but the fact that he had delivered it in person might have signaled a new era of open communication. We will never know for sure. Four days later, Lincoln was dead.

Although he grew ambivalent about which forms of expression were most proper, Lincoln's brilliant writing ultimately transcended time and tradition. Ultimately, the greatest writers of his age offered unalloyed admiration. Harriet Beecher Stowe, whose own writing had helped awaken the nation to the corrosive evil of slavery, maintained that Lincoln's words were "worthy to be inscribed in gold." And Leo Tolstoy judged that Lincoln "aspired to be divine—and he was." A century later, literary critic Edmund Wilson, no Lincoln admirer, allowed himself to admit that, "Alone among American presidents, it is possible to imagine Lincoln, grown up in a different milieu, becoming a distinguished writer of a not merely political kind."[20]

That, in the end, he never spoke aloud some of the greatest words for which he is remembered never seemed to bother Lincoln. "Speech alone, valuable as it ever has been," he declared as early as 1859, "has not involved the condition of the world much. . . . *Writing* . . . is the great invention of the world."[21]

Lincoln once declared, "I shall never be old enough to speak without embarrassment when I have nothing to talk about."[22] The fact that he had so much to say made him one of America's greatest writers, if not always its most peripatetic speakers. "Men should say nothing for which they would not be responsible through time and eternity," he reminded Congress in late 1862. The man who knew, as he put it in that same message, that he could not "escape history" found it prudent to escape the risks of extemporaneous oratory even as he crafted one of the great literary canons of his age.[23] In his own way, constrained by tradition but ennobled by his passion for freedom and democracy, he should be remembered not only as the Great Emancipator but the original "Great Communicator." This collection more than justifies that designation.

As Winston Churchill had noted, Lincoln's rhetoric emanated from "the depths of his being." But it did so with surprising rarity . . . every occasion so precious it made each sentence worth recalling to the ages, so said literary critics like Harriet Beecher Stowe, Walt Whitman, and Edmund Wilson to Churchill, and to all the students of rhetoric who have worked to understand—perhaps even to emulate—Lincoln's astonishing power with words.

In looking back at the record—it cannot be denied that as president, Lincoln wrote often but spoke seldom. As Churchill might have put it, never has so much reputation been acknowledged by so many for words so few—maybe not a bad rule for guaranteeing both literary and political immortality.

Endnotes

1. Winston S. Churchill, *History of the English-Speaking Peoples* (New York: Barnes & Noble, 1990), vol. 4, p. 171.

2. *London Times*, October 7, 1862.

3. Reprinted in Saul K. Padover, ed., *Karl Marx on America and the Civil War* (New York: McGraw-Hill, 1972), pp. 222–223.

4. *New York Tribune*, August 20, 1862.

5. Greeley wrote these words around 1870, but they were not published until Joel Benton presented them in the *Century Magazine* in July 1891. The essay was reprinted in Rufus Rockwell Wilson, ed., *Lincoln Among His Friends: A Sheaf of Intimate Memories* (Caldwell, Idaho: Caxton Printers, 1942), pp. 455–456.

6. Quoted in Stefan Lorant, *Lincoln: A Picture Story of His Life*, rev. ed. (New York: W. W. Norton, 1969), p. 159.

7. Quoted in Francis B. Carpenter, *Six Months at the White House: The Story of a Picture* (New York: Hurd & Houghton, 1866), p. 22.

8. For examples of these anodyne speeches, see Harold Holzer, *Lincoln President-Elect* (New York: Simon & Schuster, 2008), pp. 305–401.

9. Abraham Lincoln to Truman Smith, November 10, 1860, and to Nathaniel P. Paschall, November 16, 1860, in Roy P. Basler, ed., *The Collected Works of Abraham Lincoln* (New Brunswick, NJ: Rutgers University Press, 1953–55) vol. 4, pp.138, 139–40.

10. Remarks to the New Jersey State Senate, Trenton, February 21, 1861, and at Independence Hall, Philadelphia, February 22, 1861, in *Collected Works of Lincoln*, vol. 4, pp,. 236, 240.

11. For recollections of his White House routine—what Lincoln called his "public opinion baths" and his secretary called the "Beggar's Opera," see Harold Holzer, ed., *Dear Mr. Lincoln: Letters to the President* (New York: AddisonWesley, 1993), p. 4.

12. Remarks at Frederick, Maryland, October 4, 1862; and to a crowd of well-wishers at Pittsburgh, February 14, 1861, *Collected Works of Lincoln*, vol. 5, pp. 208, 450.

13. Lincoln to Isaac M. Schermerhorn, September 12, 1864, *Collected Works of Lincoln*, vol. 8, p. 2. The letter appears on pp. 1–2.

14. Lincoln to James C. Conkling, August 20, 1863, *Collected Works of Lincoln*, vol. 6, p. 399.

15. Lincoln to Conkling, August 37, 1863, ibid., vol. 6, p. 414.

16. Joseph Ignatius Gilbert, "Lincoln in 1861; Lincoln in 1863; Lincoln at Washington," lecture at the 19th annual convention of the National Shorthand Reporters' Association, orig. pub. 1871, reprinted in the *Chicago Tribune* as "I Reported the Gettysburg Address," November 19, 1878.

17. Remarks at Jersey City as transcribed and published in the *New York Times*, June 26, 1862, *Collected Works of Lincoln*, vol. 5, p. 284.

18. David Wills to Abraham Lincoln, November 2, 1863, Lincoln Papers, Library of Congress.

19. Quoted in Lorant, *Lincoln,* p. 205.

20. Quoted in Mario M. Cuomo and Harold Holzer, eds., *Lincoln on Democracy* (New York: HarperCollins, 1990), p. xxxiv.

21. Lecture on Discoveries and Inventions, ca. 1858–1859, *Collected Works of Lincoln*, vol. 3, pp. 359–360.

22. Quoted in Lois J. Einhorn, *Abraham Lincoln the Orator: Penetrating the Lincoln Legend* (Westport, CT: Greenwood Press, 1992), p. 17.

23. Annual Message to Congress, December 1, 1862, *Collected Works of Lincoln*, vol. 5, pp. 535, 537.

PROLOGUE

Abraham Lincoln is one of the most paradoxical figures in American history. A man known for his affability and mild-mannered personality, Lincoln led the nation with a remarkably firm hand and an almost preternaturally steady vision through its most turbulent and bloody period. "Father Abraham," "Honest Abe," "The Great Emancipator"—Lincoln has been mythologized as only a martyred leader could be. Yet for many, he was a flawed and reluctant hero, forced by circumstances into his role as the liberator of black Americans. For others, he remains a symbol of government overreach and oppression, and for a smaller subset of these, something even more heinous: the man responsible for the hundreds of thousands of Americans killed and maimed in a brutal war of aggression.

It cannot be disputed that Lincoln's rise to power was a uniquely American phenomenon. Despite having almost no formal education (and with a youth spent performing manual labor in a rough-hewn rural environment) and being physically unprepossessing and awkward, Lincoln rose to become an influential political leader and an epoch-defining president of a rising world power. This could not have happened anywhere else, and perhaps at no other time. In the words of the writer H. G. Wells, "He stands for your equality of opportunity, for the right and the chance of the child of the humblest home to reach the highest place. His simplicity, his humor, his patience, his deep abiding optimism, based on the conviction that right will prevail and that things must work themselves out—all these seem to typify the best that you have to give."[1] The fact that Lincoln emerged as one of the deepest and clearest thinkers and one of the most forceful leaders in American political history was, to say the least, highly improbable.

In fact, Lincoln made a career—a strategy—of being underestimated. Stephen Douglas learned quickly what a formidable foe he faced in Lincoln from the time the Little Giant, already a renowned orator, first publicly jousted with Lincoln in Bloomington, Indiana, in 1854 (though not yet on the same stage). Lincoln humiliated Douglas by quoting his words praising the Missouri Compromise, forged several years earlier, allowing the crowd to identify the holder of this now abandoned and disparaged point of view, to great comic effect.

Douglas did not repeat that mistake in the famous series of debates with Lincoln in the 1858 U.S. Senate race in Illinois, nor did Lincoln succeed in winning Douglas's seat in the Senate. Perhaps this is why the Republican elites, including the New Yorker William Seward and the Ohioan Salmon Chase, failed to recognize what a canny leader the newly elected president was when he took office in 1861, believing they could easily bend Lincoln to their will, if not crush him outright. Speaking at a funeral service for Lincoln in April 1865, the writer and philosopher Ralph Waldo Emerson commented on Lincoln's canniness:

> He offered no shining qualities at the first encounter; he did not offend by superiority. He had a face and a manner which disarmed suspicion, which inspired confidence, which confirmed good will. . . . his broad good-humor, running easily into jocular talk . . . enabled him to keep his secret; to meet every kind of man and every rank in society; to take off the edge of the severest decisions; to mask his own purpose and sound his companion; and to catch with true instinct the temper of every company he addressed.[2]

No less a political thinker than Karl Marx wrote in 1863:

> The figure of Lincoln is *sui generis* in the annals of history. No initiative, no idealistic eloquence, no buskin, no historic drapery. He always presents the most important act in the most insignificant form possible. . . . The most awesome decrees, which will always remain historically remarkable, that he hurls at the enemy all resemble, and are intended to resemble, the trite summonses that one lawyer sends to an opposing lawyer, the legal chicaneries and pettifogging stipulations of an *actiones juris.*[3]

Marx may accurately describe Lincoln's political strategy and his method of governance, yet one of the most surprising and closely examined aspects of Lincoln's life, given his upbringing and education, is that he was such an accomplished and polished writer. In fact, Lincoln's prose—he wrote verse throughout his life as well—is in many ways the defining characteristic of his presidency.

No American political leader before or since Lincoln has used the written and spoken word as effectively to gauge and alter the psyche of the nation, to provide a sense of mission, and, especially, a spiritual and moral purpose in moving the country forward. Lincoln's homely appearance and self-deprecating manner masked a keen intellect that had been fueled by the voracious appetite for reading and for knowledge of an autodidact. He had an unmatched gift for clarity and for expressing complicated ideas in simple language, often using homespun analogies to illustrate his point. Lincoln wrote in "a prose so lucid to read it is like looking a hundred feet through clear water," wrote the historian Fred Kaplan.[4] And it was his "apartness," his "detachment," that was the source of both his clarity and power over his friends and foes alike. "Had he not, as president, towered in mind and will over his cabinet," the historian Jacques Barzun asserted, "they would have crushed or used him without remorse . . . During his life, their dominant feeling toward him was exasperation with him for making them feel baffled. They could not bring him down to their reach."[5]

Humor, both spoken and written, was a weapon that Lincoln used to particular effect. His abilities as a storyteller and, especially, as a mimic were well known and highly appreciated by his friends and associates during his lifetime. He could be cruel as a mimic, especially if he felt he had been affronted or treated unfairly. But, more frequently, his humor would be used to defuse otherwise tense or difficult situations. "Effective humor, both in writing and speech, he was later to believe, had the virtue of being cathartic, an antidote to the weighty world, not an escape but a restorative," observed the historian Fred Kaplan when describing Lincoln's childhood reading.[6] Lincoln's detachment and his chronic existential self-doubt undergirded a sense of humor that was as profound as it was disarming and funny. One historian recounts that "when a delegation, which [Lincoln] had sent to Stanton with orders to grant their request, returned and reported that not only had Stanton refused to do so, but had actually called Lincoln a fool for sending such an order, Lincoln, with mock astonishment, inquired: 'Did Stanton call me a fool?'—and, upon being reassured upon that point, remarked: 'Well, I guess I had better go over and see Stanton about this. Stanton is usually right.'"[7]

Indeed, it can be said that Lincoln's sense of irony, coupled with his frequent and unselfconscious use of colloquial language and stories led directly to a tradition in American humor writing embodied by Mark Twain and Will Rogers—a shift to "vernacular rhythms," as Garry Wills described it in *Lincoln at Gettysburg*.[8]

For a man who never attended church regularly, and felt compelled to defend himself against charges of "infidelity" (a term which at that time signified straying from religious belief as opposed to the conjugal bed; see p. 26), Lincoln succeeded brilliantly in grounding his opposition to slavery in moral and religious terms. No contemporary theologian had so powerfully and economically placed the struggle against slavery in the context of humanity's fate before God as Lincoln did in, among other places, his second inaugural address (p. 206). And it was not simply political posturing; in his own private ruminations, he pondered the question of God's will with great seriousness (p. 150).

Opposition to slavery and relations between the races are at the crux of Lincoln's presidency. Though his writings reveal his sense of revulsion regarding slavery on moral grounds from a very early age, Lincoln's views on the black race were very much in keeping with those of a white Kentucky man of the mid-nineteenth century for most, if not all, of his life. That "all men are created equal," he argued, is an indisputable fact, but he hastened to add that they are not created equal in all ways. He easily indulged the views of his audiences who were aghast at the idea of the "amalgamation" of the races, as the mixing of the races was then called. He was known to tell overtly racist jokes and stories in private (and occasionally in public), though his "personal dealings with blacks did not reveal prejudice."[9]

Lincoln was clear from the outset of his presidency that he viewed the preservation of the Union as his primary objective. His opposition to slavery was confined to preventing its expansion into the territories. In his view, there was no constitutional basis for outlawing slavery in the states where it was already legal, and he assured Southern and border state voters that he had no intention of doing so. They ignored him.

Lincoln opposed citizenship for freed blacks, and, for a time, backed the idea of repatriating freed blacks into colonies like the one in Liberia, and envisioned founding a new one in Central America. As late as August 1862, he invited a committee of free black men to the White House and tried (and, unsurprisingly, failed) to convince them of the advantages of colonization (p. 137).

It was not until the Emancipation Proclamation went into effect in January 1863 that Lincoln began to seriously contemplate giving the elective franchise to at least some black citizens. And perhaps moved by the many instances of bravery, leadership, and sacrifice among black recruits in the Union army, Lincoln began to champion the idea of full citizenship for blacks near the end of his life.

Eleven years after Lincoln's death, Frederick Douglass, who had been a harsh critic of Lincoln's early in his presidency, and later a champion, summed up the fallen president this way:

> Our faith in him was often taxed and strained to the uttermost, but it never failed. When he tarried long in the mountain; when he strangely told us that we were the cause of the war; when he still more strangely told us to leave the

land in which we were born; when he refused to employ our arms in defense of the Union; when, after accepting our services as colored soldiers, he refused to retaliate when we were murdered as colored prisoners [Lincoln eventually reversed himself on this, p. 178]; when he told us he would save the Union if he could with slavery; when he revoked the proclamation of emancipation of General Frémont [see p. 123]; when he refused to remove the commander of the Army of the Potomac, who was more zealous in his efforts to protect slavery than suppress rebellion; when we saw this, and more, we were at times stunned, grieved and greatly bewildered; but our hearts believed while they ached and bled.

. . . Had he put the abolition of slavery before the salvation of the Union, he would have inevitably driven from him a powerful class of the American people, and rendered resistance to rebellion impossible. Viewed from the genuine abolition ground, Mr. Lincoln seemed tardy, cold, dull, and indifferent: but measuring him by the sentiment of his country, a sentiment he was bound as a statesman to consult, he was swift, zealous, radical, and determined.[10]

It seems clear that any look at Lincoln's legacy and at Lincoln the man is destined to be subject to the political biases that we, as readers of history, bring to it—only more so for Lincoln than almost any other American leader. His presidency and the political and moral issues he grappled with throughout his life rest squarely on the fault lines of American history, lines that were established, and to some extent obscured, by the founders, and that continue to underlie the political discourse of today: the issues of race and of the appropriate role of the federal government in mandating state and even individual conduct.

Even before his assassination, Lincoln was a beloved figure for most Americans who were not reflexively opposed to him, principally because he was one of them, and appeared to remain unaffected by his powerful office. He thought it was his responsibility to welcome citizens into the White House, for example, and he regularly sent notes of gratitude to groups of "serenaders" who would sing outside the White House to show support for the president (p. 153). One gets the feeling that they thought he needed cheering up, and they were probably right. Lincoln's deliberate manner, his verbal and written clarity, his vernacular wit, and his sense of moral purpose made his supporters feel that this man, in the end, was a decent human being. The fact that he died on Good Friday—April 15, 1865—only served to validate a belief about Lincoln that many people already held.

One way in which to assess Lincoln's accomplishments is by examining their net result: the Union was preserved, slavery was abolished, hatred and retribution gave way to healing as well as could be expected after such a brutal war. First and foremost, it was Lincoln's clarion words, spoken and written, legalistic, humble, commanding, simple, humorous, poetic, and spiritual, that nudged American discourse closer to the modern era and brought Americans around to the "better angels of their nature," at least for a time.

ACKNOWLEDGMENTS

Thanks to J.P. Leventhal, publisher of Black Dog & Leventhal, for this opportunity. To Lisa Tenaglia, my smart and indefatigable editor, for never failing to make the book better. And to Kathryn Williams for taking on the photo research in the face of impossible deadlines.

Profound gratitude to Harold Holzer for sharing his vast expertise and knowledge of all things Lincoln—and for vetting my text and writing the thoughtful foreword.

I am grateful to the Abraham Lincoln Association for their kind permission to reproduce Lincoln's words here.

My thanks to my wife, Megan, for encouraging me to do what I love; and to my daughter, Stella, who inspires me to see everything with fresh eyes.

NOTES ON THE TEXT

This collection of Lincoln's writings comes primarily from the eight volumes of Lincoln's *Collected Works* edited by Roy P. Basler and published by Rutgers University Press in 1953. The complete collection is now available online via the University of Michigan Digital Library (http://quod.lib.umich.edu/l/lincoln/), which is an invaluable resource well worth visiting.

I am grateful to the Abraham Lincoln Association for their kind permission to reproduce Lincoln's words here.

I have preserved Lincoln's spelling and grammar in order to retain his authentic voice and the sense of the period.

I. "Too Familiar with Disappointment to Be Much Chagrined"

The first known photo of Lincoln, a daguerreotype by the Springfield photographer Nicholas Shepherd, taken ca. 1846 or 1847.

The one-room, dirt-floor log cabin in Hardin County, Kentucky, where Abraham Lincoln was born on February 12, 1809.

Abraham Lincoln's childhood and early life are so unusually fraught with hardship and deprivation that it is worth looking beyond the "born-in-a-log-cabin-on-the-Kentucky-frontier, became-a-rail-splitter" mythology that is so familiar to anyone who has attended primary school in the United States. Prior to his birth, the family had a direct and visceral experience of one of the less appealing aspects of frontier life: Lincoln's grandfather (and namesake, Abraham) was shot dead by a Native American rifleman in front of Lincoln's father, Thomas, and his two other sons. Thomas's brother, Mordecai, shot the murderer dead, saving the six-year-old Thomas's life, and forever shaping his worldview.

Lincoln's younger brother, also named Thomas, died in infancy. His mother, Nancy Hanks Lincoln (born around 1794), died of "milk sick" (caused by drinking milk from a cow that had eaten poisonous plants) in 1818, the same year that Lincoln turned nine, and was kicked in the head by a horse (he was thought, briefly, to be dead). His older sister, Sarah, died in childbirth at age twenty-one in 1828. Lincoln was not yet twenty. The family had been so poor during Lincoln's childhood—relocating from Kentucky to Indiana to Illinois—and the need for his labor to clear and work the land so great, that the totality of his schooling was about a year. Though Thomas Lincoln remarried a woman whom the younger Lincoln revered, the future president did not have much regard for his father. In 1851, when notified by letter that his father was dying, Lincoln supplied a dubious excuse for being unable to visit, adding, "Say to him that if we could meet now it is doubtful whether it would not be more painful than pleasant" (p. 40).

In 1835, when Lincoln was almost twenty-six, the woman whom many believe to have been the great love of his life, Ann Rutledge, died of typhoid fever. Never a ladies' man, Lincoln subsequently engaged in a halfhearted courtship of Mary Owens, the twenty-eight-year-old sister of a friend. She rejected his

The Rail Splitter, painted by Jean Leon Gerome Ferris in the early twentieth century, shows an idealized view of the future president's origins.

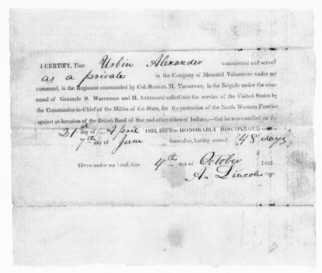

Discharge certificate for Private Urbin Alexander, signed by Captain Abraham Lincoln on October 4, 1832.

proposal of marriage in 1837. He experienced bouts of depression (then known as "hypochondria") during this period, in the mid-1830s. Hypochondria visited him again in the bleak winter of 1840–1841, when Lincoln briefly ended his courtship of Mary Todd. His depression was so profound that he was forced to take a leave from his position in the state legislature, writing to his colleague John Stuart, "I am now the most miserable man living. If what I feel were equally distributed to the whole human family, there would not be one cheerful face on the earth" (p. 17)." Lincoln recovered and resumed his courtship of Mary Todd, marrying her in 1842.

It was clear from early in his life that Lincoln was a striver. His law partner, William Herndon, described Lincoln's ambition as "a little engine that knew no rest."[1] With no education, training, or prospects, Lincoln, at age sixteen, began to get work as a boatman and farmhand, traveling as far as New Orleans, eventually building a flatboat with his stepbrother, John Johnston. In 1830, he made what is generally believed to be his first foray into politics, delivering a speech arguing for improving navigation on the Sangamon River.

When the Black Hawk War broke out in 1832, Lincoln volunteered and was elected company captain, an acknowledgment of his leadership abilities. He was extremely proud of attaining this high rank, as he noted in his campaign biography (p. 82). He obtained an appointment for himself as postmaster of New Salem (see letter, pp. 10, 65), and became a surveyor.

In 1832, Lincoln lost his first election to become a member of the Illinois General Assembly (see p. 9 for his humble and humorous campaign speech), but was elected two years later to that body. Meanwhile, he studied law, earning his license to practice in 1836. After successfully campaigning to have the state capital moved from Vandalia to Springfield, Lincoln left New Salem and relocated to the new capital, taking up lodging with Joshua Speed, who was to become his closest friend (see p. 19).

Lincoln was elected to the U.S. House of Representatives in 1846, serving one term from 1848–1850 before returning to Illinois to focus on his law practice, which consisted principally of property disputes. But Lincoln remained engaged in politics, delivering speeches, writing editorials, endorsing candidates, and making notes to himself, testing and refining his political views and his power to move people with his words.

Excerpts from Lincoln's boyhood copybook (1824–1826)

Abraham Lincoln
his hand and pen
he will be good but
god knows When
Time What an emty vaper
tis and days how swift they are swift as an indian arr[ow]
Meter
fly on like a shooting star the presant moment Just [is here]

then slides away in h[as]te that we [can] never say they['re ours]
but [only say] th[ey]'re past
Abraham Lincoln is my nam[e]
And with my pen I wrote the same
I wrote in both hast[e] and speed
and left it here for fools to read[2]

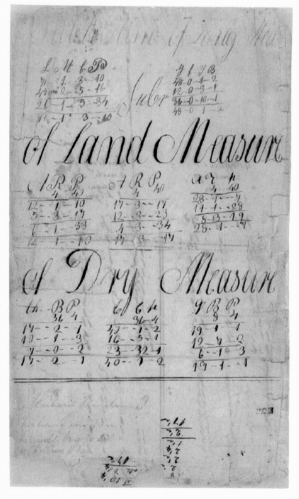

In the autobiography he wrote for the 1860 presidential campaign (see p. 81), Lincoln claimed that his formal schooling amounted to less than one year in total. Resources on the prairie frontier, such as textbooks and paper, were scarce, so students often used boards, which they could shave and reuse, to copy down math problems and practice writing. Lincoln found a few sheets of paper and stitched them together to form a small mathematical notebook, pages of which are shown here. On the lower left-hand corner of the page shown at left, one can faintly make out the humorous ditty that he wrote about himself.

Abraham Lincoln
his hand and pen
he will be good but
god knows When

If 3 ℔ of ginger cost 3s what
cost 26 lb ————————

(No 2)

26
3
3) 7 8
20) 2 66
2 0
6

W. H. Herndon

If 2 oz of silk cost 2S 6D
what cost 7 LB Answer 7 L

2 —— 2 6 —— 7
12   16
30   4 2
          7
         1 1 2
          3 0
     2) 3 3 6 0
    20) 1 6 8 0   7 L

1 4
4 8
1 4 4
7 2
4) 8 6 4
12) 2 1 6
1 8 shilling

If 1 ℔ of sugar cost
what cost 1 Cwt ans
1 £ 17 S 8 4d ———

1 — 4 —— 1 1 2
1 1 2
12) 4 4 8
20) 3 7 — 4d
answer 1 £ 17 S —— 4d

If an Cwt of sugar cost
2 £ 12 S what coste
16 —— 2 £ 12 S 1 lb
20
5 2
1 2
1 0 4
9 2
112) 6 2 4 [5
5 6 0
6 4
4
64) 2 5 6 (2
2 2 4

answer

... proportion
... proportion is when more requires more or
... quires less
... t do you mean by more requires more ——
... ore requires more is when the third is greater
... the first and therefore requires the fourth term
... greater than the second in the same proportio...
... hat do you mean by less requires less
... requires less is when third term is less than
... first and therefore requires the fourth
... to be less than the second in the like
... rtion
... ow is the fourth term found in
... t proportion
... multiplying the 2nd and 3rd
... gether and dividing that
... by the first term

To the people of Sangamo County, "I have been too familiar with disappointments to be very much chagrined."

Lincoln was running for a seat in the state legislature and offered a platform addressing local issues before coming to his conclusion, below.

New Salem, March 9, 1832

. . . Every man is said to have his peculiar ambition. Whether it be true or not, I can say for one that I have no other so great as that of being truly esteemed of my fellow men, by rendering myself worthy of their esteem. How far I shall succeed in gratifying this ambition, is yet to be developed. I am young and unknown to many of you. I was born and have ever remained in the most

In 1833, Lincoln was appointed by the Sangamon County surveyor to be his deputy in spite of the fact that the twenty-four-year-old Lincoln had no knowledge or qualifications whatsoever. Already the New Salem postmaster, Lincoln very quickly taught himself the trade and procured the necessary equipment on credit. Pictured below are Lincoln's notes, made on behalf of the widow Rhoda Hart, in legal proceedings involving the sale of her deceased husband's land against a competing family member's claims. Lincoln and Hart prevailed in the case.

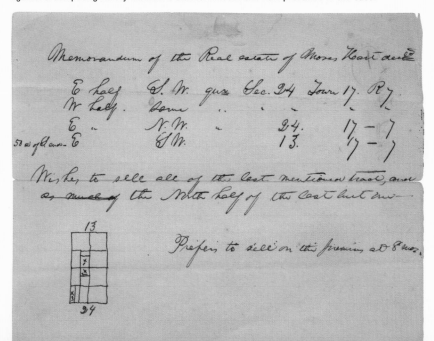

humble walks of life. I have no wealthy or popular relations to recommend me. My case is thrown exclusively upon the independent voters of this county, and if elected they will have conferred a favor upon me, for which I shall be unremitting in my labors to compensate. But if the good people in their wisdom shall see fit to keep me in the background, I have been too familiar with disappointments to be very much chagrined.[3]

Letter to George Spears (1836), "you choose to wound my feelings . . ."

Lincoln's humorous effort to collect overdue postage as the New Salem postmaster from one of the frontier city's leading citizens.

Mr. Spears:

At your request I send you a receipt for the postage on your paper. I am somewhat surprised at your request. I will, however, comply with it. The law requires newspaper postage to be paid in advance, and now that I have waited a full year you choose to wound my feelings by insinuating that unless you get a receipt I will probably make you pay it again.[4]

Letter to Colonel Robert Allen, responding to a political smear, "my opinion of your veracity will not permit me for a moment to doubt that you at least believed what you said."

Robert Allen was a Springfield businessman whom Lincoln knew and considered a friend.

New Salem, June 21, 1836

Dear Colonel:—I am told that during my absence last week you passed through this place, and stated publicly that you were in possession of a fact or facts which, if known to the public, would entirely destroy the prospects of N. W. Edwards [Ninian Edwards, a Whig ally of Lincoln's and the husband of Mary

Todd Lincoln's sister Elizabeth] and myself at the ensuing election; but that, through favor to us, you should forbear to divulge them. No one has needed favors more than I, and, generally, few have been less unwilling to accept them; but in this case favor to me would be injustice to the public, and therefore I must beg your pardon for declining it. That I once had the confidence of the people of Sangamon, is sufficiently evident; and if I have since done anything, either by design or misadventure, which if known would subject me to a forfeiture of that confidence, he that knows of that thing, and conceals it, is a traitor to his country's interest.

I find myself wholly unable to form any conjecture of what fact or facts, real or supposed, you spoke; but my opinion of your veracity will not permit me for a moment to doubt that you at least believed what you said. I am flattered with the personal regard you manifested for me; but I do hope that, on more mature reflection, you will view the public interest as a paramount consideration, and therefore determine to let the worst come. I here assure you that the candid statement of facts on your part, however low it may sink me, shall never break the tie of personal friendship between us. I wish an answer to this, and you are at liberty to publish both, if you choose.[5]

Letters to Mary Owens, "You would have to be poor . . ."

Owens was a wealthy Kentuckian, the sister of a married friend, to whom Lincoln halfheartedly proposed marriage.

Springfield, May 7, 1837

Friend Mary:—I have commenced two letters to send you before this, both of which displeased me before I got half done, and so I tore them up. The first I thought was not serious enough, and the second was on the other extreme. I shall send this, turn out as it may.

This thing of living in Springfield is rather a dull business, after all; at least it is so to me. I am quite as lonesome here as I ever was anywhere in my life. I have been spoken to by but one woman since I have been here, and should not have been by her if she could have avoided it. I've never been to church yet, and probably shall not be soon. I stay away because I am conscious I should not know how to behave myself.

I am often thinking of what we said about your coming to live at Springfield. I am afraid you would not be satisfied. There is a great deal of flourishing about in carriages here, which it would be your doom to see without sharing it. You would have to be poor, without the means of hiding your poverty. Do you believe you could bear that patiently? Whatever woman may cast her lot with mine, should any ever do so, it is my intention to do all in my power to make her happy and contented; and there is nothing I can imagine that would make me more unhappy than to fail in the effort. I know I should be much happier with you than the way I am, provided I saw no signs of discontent in you. What you have said to me may have been in the way of jest, or I may have misunderstood you. If so, then let it be forgotten; if otherwise, I much wish you would think seriously before you decide. What I have said I will most positively abide by, provided you wish it. My opinion is that you had better not do it. You have not been accustomed to hardship, and it may be more severe than you now imagine. I know you are capable of thinking correctly on any subject, and if you deliberate maturely upon this subject before you decide, then I am willing to abide your decision.

You must write me a good long letter after you get this. You have nothing else to do, and though it might not seem interesting to you after you had written it, it would be a good deal of company to me in this "busy wilderness." Tell your sister I don't want to hear any more about selling out and moving. That gives me the "hypo" whenever I think of it.[6]

Lincoln met Mary Owens (1808-1877) when she visited her sister, Elizabeth Abell, in New Salem in 1833. Lincoln's senior by a year, Owens came from a well-to-do Kentucky family, and was as well educated and refined as Lincoln was the opposite. Lincoln told Elizabeth that if her sister returned, he would marry her. She did, perhaps a little too hastily for Lincoln. The two had an affectionate but prickly relationship that began with a promise of marriage and ended with bad feelings on both sides, and Lincoln ungallantly confided to a New England confidante that Mary was too old and plump to wed—when in fact it was she who rejected him!

Second letter to Mary Owens, "If it suits you best not to answer this, farewell."

Springfield, Aug. 16, 1837

Friend Mary: You will no doubt think it rather strange that I should write you a letter on the same day on which we parted, and I can only account for it by supposing that seeing you lately makes me think of you more than usual; while at our late meeting we had but few expressions of thoughts. You must know that I cannot see you, or think of you, with entire indifference; and yet it may be that you are mistaken in regard to what my real feelings toward you are.

If I knew you were not, I should not have troubled you with this letter. Perhaps any other man would know enough without information; but I consider it my peculiar right to plead ignorance, and your bounden duty to allow the plea.

I want in all cases to do right; and most particularly so in all cases with women.

I want, at this particular time, more than any thing else to do right with you; and if I knew it would be doing right, as I rather suspect it would, to let you alone I would do it. And, for the purpose of making the matter as plain as possible, I now say that you can drop the subject, dismiss your thoughts (if you ever had any) from me for ever and leave this letter unanswered without calling forth one accusing murmur from me. And I will even go further and say that, if it will add anything to your comfort or peace of mind to do so, it is my sincere wish that you should. Do not understand by this that I wish to cut your acquaintance. I mean no such thing. What I do wish is that our further acquaintance shall depend upon yourself. If such further acquaintance would contribute nothing to your happiness, I am sure it would not to mine. If you feel yourself in any degree bound to me, I am now willing to release you, provided you wish it; while on the other hand I am willing and even anxious to bind you faster if I can be convinced that it will, in any considerable degree, add to your happiness. This, indeed, is the whole question with me. Nothing would make me more miserable than to believe you miserable, nothing more happy than to know you were so.

In what I have now said, I think I cannot be misunderstood; and to make myself understood is the only object of this letter.

If it suits you best not to answer this, farewell. A long life and a merry one attend you. But, if you conclude to write back, speak as plainly as I do. There can neither be harm nor danger in saying to me anything you think, just in the manner you think it. My respects to your sister.[7]

Lincoln's August 16, 1837, letter to Mary Owens. She never responded.

Letter to Eliza Browning, "I can never be satisfied with any one who would be blockhead enough to have me."

Lincoln explains his failed courtship of Mary Owens to Eliza Browning, the wife of Lincoln's Illinois political ally (and Black Hawk War comrade-in-arms) Orville Hickman Browning. Mrs. Browning became a confidante of Lincoln's.

Springfield, April 1, 1838

Dear Madam:—Without apologizing for being egotistical, I shall make the history of so much of my life as has elapsed since I saw you the subject of this letter.

. . . It was . . . in the autumn of 1836 that a married lady of my acquaintance, and who was a great friend of mine, being about to pay a visit to her father and other relatives residing in Kentucky, proposed to me that on her return she would bring a sister of hers with her on condition that I would engage to become her brother-in-law with all convenient despatch. I, of course, accepted the proposal, for you know I could not have done otherwise had I really been averse to it; but privately, between you and me, I was most confoundedly well pleased with the project. I had seen the said sister some three years before, thought her intelligent and agreeable, and saw no good objection to plodding life through hand in hand with her. Time passed on; the lady took her journey and in due time returned, sister in company, sure enough. This astonished me a little, for it appeared to me that her coming so readily showed that she was a trifle too willing, but on reflection it occurred to me that she might have been prevailed on by her married sister to come without anything concerning me ever having been mentioned to her, and so I concluded that if no other objection presented itself, I would consent to waive this. All this occurred to me on hearing of her arrival in the neighborhood—for, be it remembered, I had not yet seen her, except about three years previous, as above mentioned. In a few days we had an interview, and, although I had seen her before, she did not look as my imagination had pictured her. I knew she was over-size, but she now appeared a fair match for Falstaff. I knew she was called an "old maid," and I felt no doubt of the truth of at least half of the appellation, but now, when I beheld her, I could not for my life avoid thinking of my mother; and this, not from withered features,—for her skin was too full of fat to permit of its contracting into wrinkles,—but from her want of teeth, weather-beaten appearance in general, and from a kind of notion that ran in my head that nothing could have commenced at the size of infancy and reached her present bulk in less than thirty-five or forty years; and in short, I was not at all pleased with her. But what could I do? I had told her sister that I would take her for better or for worse, and I made a point of honor and conscience in all things to stick to my word especially if others had been induced to act on it which in this case I had no doubt they had, for I was now fairly convinced that no other man on earth would have her, and hence the conclusion that they were bent on holding me to my bargain.

"Well," thought I, "I have said it, and, be the consequences what they may, it shall not be my fault if I fail to do it." At once I determined to consider her my wife; and, this done, all my powers of discovery were put to work in search of perfections in her which might be fairly set off against her defects. I tried to imagine her handsome, which, but for her unfortunate corpulency, was actually true. Exclusive of this no woman that I have ever seen has a finer face. I also tried to convince myself that the mind was much more to be valued than the person; and in this she was not inferior, as I could discover, to any with whom I had been acquainted.

Shortly after this, without coming to any positive understanding with her, I set out for Vandalia, when and where you first saw me. During my stay there I had letters from her which did not change my opinion of either her intellect or intention, but on the contrary confirmed it in both.

All this while, although I was fixed, "firm as the surge-repelling rock," in my resolution, I found I was continually repenting the rashness which had led me to make it. Through life, I have been in no bondage, either real or imaginary, from the thraldom of which I so much desired to be free. After my return home, I saw nothing to change my opinions of her in any particular. She was the same, and so was I. I now spent my time in planning how I might get along through life after my contemplated change of circumstances should have taken place, and how I might procrastinate the evil day for a time, which I really dreaded as much, perhaps more, than an Irishman does the halter.

After all my suffering upon this deeply interesting subject, here I am, wholly, unexpectedly, completely, out of the "scrape"; and now I want to know if you can guess how I got out of it—out, clear, in every sense of the term; no violation of word, honor, or conscience. I don't believe you can guess, and so I might as well tell you at once. As the lawyer says, it was done in the manner following, to wit: After I had delayed the matter as long as I thought I could in honor do (which, by the way, had brought me round into the last fall), I concluded I might as well bring it to a consummation without further delay; and so I mustered my resolution, and made the proposal to her direct; but, shocking to relate, she answered, No. At first I supposed she did it through an affectation of modesty, which I thought but ill became her under the peculiar circumstances of her case; but on my renewal of the charge, I found she repelled it with greater firmness than before. I tried it again and again but with the same success, or rather with the same want of success.

I finally was forced to give it up; at which I very unexpectedly found myself mortified almost beyond endurance. I was mortified, it seemed to me, in a hundred different ways. My vanity was deeply wounded by the reflection that I had been too stupid to discover her intentions, and at the same time never doubting that I understood them perfectly, and also that she, whom I had taught myself to believe nobody else would have, had actually rejected me with all my fancied greatness. And, to cap the whole, I then for the first time began to suspect that I was really a little in love with her. But let it all go. I'll try and outlive it. Others have been made fools of by the girls, but this can never with truth be said of me. I most emphatically in this instance, made a fool of myself. I have now come to the conclusion never again to think of marrying, and for this reason: I can never be satisfied with any one who would be blockhead enough to have me.

When you receive this, write me a long yarn about something to amuse me. Give my respects to Mr. Browning.[8]

Letter to John T. Stuart, "I am now the most miserable man living."

Stuart was a favorite cousin of Mary Todd Lincoln's and was Lincoln's law partner in Springfield from 1837 to 1841.

Springfield, Ills., Jany. 23rd, 1841
Dear Stuart:

Yours of the 3rd. Inst. is recd. & I proceed to answer it as well as I can, tho' from the deplorable state of my mind at this time, I fear I shall give you but little satisfaction. . . . For not giving you a general summary of news, you must pardon me; it is not in my power to do so. I am now the most miserable man living. If what I feel were equally distributed to the whole human family, there would not be one cheerful face on the earth. Whether I shall ever be better I can not tell; I awfully forebode I shall not. To remain as I am is impossible; I must die or be better, it appears to me. The matter you speak of on my account, you may attend to as you say, unless you shall hear of my condition forbidding it. I say this, because

I fear I shall be unable to attend to any bussiness here, and a change of scene might help me. If I could be myself, I would rather remain at home with Judge Logan. I can write no more.[9]

The concluding page of Lincoln's January 23, 1841, letter to John T. Stuart (1807–1885). Stuart was Mary Todd Lincoln's cousin, and a friend and mentor of Lincoln. The two men had served together during the Black Hawk War, and it was Stuart who had gotten him interested in the law. Around the end of 1840, Lincoln began to have serious doubts about his relationship with Mary Todd, whom he had been courting since the previous year. Some time around January 1, 1841, he broke off the relationship with Todd, his general anxiety perhaps exacerbated by the departure of his closest friend, Joshua Speed, for new prospects in Kentucky. Prone to depression, Lincoln fell into an emotional tailspin from which it took him months to recover.

Address to the Springfield Washingtonian Temperance Society, "If you would win a man to your cause, first convince him that you are his sincere friend."

February 22, 1842

... When the conduct of men is designed to be influenced, persuasion, kind, unassuming persuasion, should ever be adopted. It is an old and a true maxim that "a drop of honey catches more flies than a gallon of gall." So with men. If you would win a man to your cause, first convince him that you are his sincere friend. Therein is a drop of honey that catches his heart, which, say what he will, is the great highroad to his reason; and which, when once gained, you will find but little trouble in convincing his judgment of the justice of your cause, if indeed that cause really be a just one. On the contrary, assume to dictate to his judgment, or to command his action, or to mark him as one to be shunned and despised, and he will retreat within himself, close all the avenues to his head and his heart; and though your cause be naked truth itself, transformed to the heaviest lance, harder than steel, and sharper than steel can be made, and though you throw it with more than herculean force and precision, you shall be no more able to pierce him than to penetrate the hard shell of a tortoise with a rye straw. Such is man, and so must he be understood by those who would lead him, even to his own best interests.[10]

Letter to Joshua F. Speed, "I must gain my confidence in my own ability to keep my resolves when they are made."

Speed took Lincoln in upon his arrival in Springfield in 1837. The two shared a bed in the apartment above Speed's general store and became lifelong friends.

Springfield, Illinois, July 4, 1842

... As to my having been displeased with your advice, surely you know better than that. I know you do, and therefore will not labor to convince you. True, that subject is painful to me; but it is not your silence, or the silence of all the world, that can make me forget it. I acknowledge the correctness of your advice too; but before I resolve to do the one thing or the other, I must gain my confidence in my own ability to keep my resolves when they are made. In that ability you know I once prided myself as the only or chief gem of my character; that gem I lost—how and where you know too well. I have not yet regained it; and until I do, I cannot trust myself in any matter of much importance. I believe now that had you understood my case at the time as well as I understand yours afterward, by the aid you would have given me I should have sailed through clear, but that does not now afford me sufficient confidence to begin that or the like of that again.

You make a kind acknowledgment of your obligations to me for your present happiness. I am pleased with that acknowledgment. But a thousand

Lincoln had met Joshua Speed (1814-1882) on the day he arrived in Springfield in April 1837, walking into the general store that Speed co-owned to buy himself a mattress, blankets, sheets, and a pillow with no money. Speed, who knew of Lincoln thanks to his political speeches, offered him credit and a share in his lodgings above the store. The two maintained a close friendship for the remainder of Lincoln's life at Springfield—though Speed, a slave owner, later came to oppose Lincoln and returned to Kentucky and politics.

times more am I pleased to know that you enjoy a degree of happiness worthy of an acknowledgment. The truth is, I am not sure that there was any merit with me in the part I took in your difficulty; I was drawn to it by a fate. If I would I could not have done less than I did. I always was superstitious; I believe God made me one of the instruments of bringing your Fanny and you together, which union I have no doubt He had fore-ordained. Whatever He designs He will do for me yet. "Stand still, and see the salvation of the Lord" is my text just now. If, as you say, you have told Fanny all, I should have no objection to her seeing this letter, but for its reference to our friend here: let her seeing it depend upon whether she has ever known anything of my affairs; and if she has not, do not let her.

I do not think I can come to Kentucky this season. I am so poor and make so little headway in the world, that I drop back in a month of idleness as much as I gain in a year's sowing. I should like to visit you again. I should like to see that "sis" of yours that was absent when I was there, though I suppose she would run away again if she were to hear I was coming.

My respects and esteem to all your friends there, and, by your permission, my love to your Fanny.[11]

Letter to Joshua Speed, "From anybody but me this would be an impudent question, not to be tolerated; but I know you will pardon it in me."

Springfield, October 4, 1842

Dear Speed:—You have heard of my duel with Shields [Lincoln had ridiculed Shields, the state auditor, in a letter published in the *Sangamo Journal* (to which Mary Todd and a friend had added an equally insulting follow-up), and Shields had challenged him to a duel, which was settled before it began], and I have now to inform you that the dueling business still rages in this city. Day before yesterday Shields challenged Butler, who accepted, and proposed fighting next morning at sunrise in Bob Allen's meadow, one hundred yards' distance, with rifles. To this Whitesides, Shields's second, said "No," because of the law. Thus ended duel No. 2. Yesterday Whitesides chose to consider himself insulted by Dr. Merryman, so sent him a kind of quasi-challenge, inviting him to meet him at the Planter's House in St. Louis on the next Friday, to settle their difficulty. Merryman made me his friend, and sent Whitesides a note, inquiring to know if he meant his note as a challenge, and if so, that he would, according to the law in such case made and provided, prescribe the terms of the meeting. Whitesides returned for answer that if Merryman would meet him at the Planter's House as desired, he would challenge him. Merryman replied in a note that he denied Whitesides's right to dictate time and place, but that he [Merryman] would waive the question of time, and meet him at Louisiana, Missouri. Upon my presenting this note to Whitesides and stating verbally its contents, he declined receiving it, saying he had business in St. Louis, and it was as near as Louisiana. Merryman then directed me to notify Whitesides that he should publish the correspondence between them, with such comments as he thought fit. This I did. Thus it stood at bedtime last night. This morning Whitesides, by his friend Shields, is praying for a new trial, on the ground that he was mistaken in Merryman's proposition to meet him at Louisiana, Missouri, thinking it was the State of Louisiana. This Merryman hoots at, and is preparing his publication; while the town is in a ferment, and a street fight somewhat anticipated.

But I began this letter not for what I have been writing, but to say something on that subject which you know to be of such infinite solicitude to me. The immense sufferings you endured from the first days of September till the middle of February you never tried to conceal from me, and I well understood. You have now been the husband of a lovely woman nearly eight months. That you are happier now than the day you married her I well know, for without you could not be living. But I have your word for it, too, and the returning elasticity of spirits which is manifested in your letters. But I want to ask a close question, "Are you now in feeling as well as judgment glad that you are married as you are?" From anybody but me this would be an impudent question, not to be tolerated; but I know you will pardon it in me. Please answer it quickly, as I am impatient to know. I have sent my love to your Fanny so often, I fear she is getting tired of it. However, I venture to tender it again.[12]

An interior view of the Hardin County cabin in which Lincoln was born, showing the fireplace and his mother's spinning jenny.

Poem: My Childhood Home I See Again

[February 25?] 1846

My childhood-home I see again,
And gladden with the view;
And still as mem'ries crowd my brain,
There's sadness in it too.
O memory! thou mid-way world
'Twixt Earth and Paradise,
Where things decayed, and loved ones lost
In dreamy shadows rise.
And freed from all that's gross or vile,
Seem hallowed, pure, and bright,
Like scenes in some enchanted isle,
All bathed in liquid light.
As distant mountains please the eye,
When twilight chases day—
As bugle-tones, that, passing by,
In distance die away—
As leaving some grand water-fall
We ling'ring, list it's roar,
So memory will hallow all
We've known, but know no more.

Now twenty years have passed away,
Since here I bid farewell
To woods, and fields, and scenes of play
And school-mates loved so well.
Where many were, how few remain
Of old familiar things!
But seeing these to mind again
The lost and absent brings.
The friends I left that parting day—
How changed, as time has sped!
Young childhood grown, strong manhood grey,
And half of all are dead.
I hear the lone survivors tell
How nought from death could save,
Till every sound appears a knell,
And every spot a grave.
I range the fields with pensive tread,
And pace the hollow rooms;
And feel (companions of the dead)
I'm living in the tombs.
A[nd] here's an object more of dread,
Than ought the grave contains—
A human-form, with reason fled,
While wretched life remains.
Poor Matthew! Once of genius bright,—
A fortune-favored child—
Now locked for aye, in mental night,
A haggard mad-man wild.
Poor Matthew! I have ne'er forgot
When first with maddened will,
Yourself you maimed, your father fought,
And mother strove to kill;
And terror spread, and neighbours ran,
Your dang'rous strength to bind;
And soon a howling crazy man,
Your limbs were fast confined.
How then you writhed and shrieked aloud,
Your bones and sinnews bared;

And fiendish on the gaping crowd,
With burning eye-balls glared.
And begged, and swore, and wept, and prayed,
With maniac laughter joined—
How fearful are the signs displayed,
By pangs that kill the mind!
And when at length, tho' drear and long,
Time soothed your fiercer woes—
How plaintively your mournful song,
Upon the still night rose.
I've heard it oft, as if I dreamed,
Far-distant, sweet, and lone;
The funeral dirge it ever seemed
Of reason dead and gone.
To drink it's strains, I've stole away,
All silently and still,
Ere yet the rising god of day
Had streaked the Eastern hill.
Air held his breath; the trees all still
Seemed sorr'wing angels round.
Their swelling tears in dew-drops fell
Upon the list'ning ground.
But this is past, and nought remains
That raised you o'er the brute.
Your mad'ning shrieks and soothing strains
Are like forever mute.
Now fare thee well: more thou the cause
Than subject now of woe.
All mental pangs, but time's kind laws,
Hast lost the power to know.
And now away to seek some scene
Less painful than the last—
With less of horror mingled in
The present and the past.
The very spot where grew the bread
That formed my bones, I see.
How strange, old field, on thee to tread,
And feel I'm part of thee![13]

Handbill replying to charges of infidelity, "I have never denied the truth of the Scriptures . . ."

July 31, 1846
To the Voters of the Seventh Congressional District
Fellow Citizens:

A charge having got into circulation in some of the neighborhoods of this District, in substance that I am an open scoffer at Christianity, I have by the advice of some friends concluded to notice the subject in this form. That I am not a member of any Christian Church, is true; but I have never denied the truth of the Scriptures; and I have never spoken with intentional disrespect of religion in general, or of any denomination of Christians in particular. It is true that in early life I was inclined to believe in what I understand is called the "Doctrine of Necessity"—that is, that the human mind is impelled to action, or held in rest by some power, over which the mind itself has no control; and I have sometimes (with one, two or three, but never publicly) tried to maintain this opinion in argument. The habit of arguing thus however-er, I have, entirely left off for more than five years. And I add here, I have always understood this same opinion to be held by several of the Christian denominations. The foregoing, is the whole truth, briefly stated, in relation to myself, upon this subject.

I do not think I could myself, be brought to support a man for office, whom I knew to be an open enemy of, and scoffer at, religion. Leaving the higher matter of eternal consequences, between him and his Maker, I still do not think any man has the right thus to insult the feelings, and injure the morals, of the community in which he may live. If, then, I was guilty of such conduct, I should blame no man who should condemn me for it; but I do blame those, whoever they may be, who falsely put such a charge in circulation against me.[14]

Poem: The Bear Hunt

[September 6, 1846?]

A wild-bear chace, didst never see?
Then hast thou lived in vain.
Thy richest bump of glorious glee,
Lies desert in thy brain.
When first my father settled here,
'Twas then the frontier line:
The panther's scream, filled night with fear
And bears preyed on the swine.
But wo for Bruin's short lived fun,
When rose the squealing cry;
Now man and horse, with dog and gun,
For vengeance, at him fly.
A sound of danger strikes his ear;
He gives the breeze a snuff:
Away he bounds, with little fear,
And seeks the tangled rough.
On press his foes, and reach the ground,
Where's left his half munched meal;
The dogs, in circles, scent around,
And find his fresh made trail.
With instant cry, away they dash,
And men as fast pursue;
O'er logs they leap, through water splash,
And shout the brisk halloo.
Now to elude the eager pack,
Bear shuns the open ground;
Th[r]ough matted vines, he shapes his track
And runs it, round and round.
The tall fleet cur, with deep-mouthed voice,
Now speeds him, as the wind;
While half-grown pup, and short-legged fice,
Are yelping far behind.
And fresh recruits are dropping in
To join the merry corps:

With yelp and yell,—a mingled din—
The woods are in a roar.
And round, and round the chace now goes,
The world's alive with fun;
Nick Carter's horse, his rider throws,
And more, Hill drops his gun.
Now sorely pressed, bear glances back,
And lolls his tired tongue;
When as, to force him from his track,
An ambush on him sprung.
Across the glade he sweeps for flight,
And fully is in view.
The dogs, new-fired, by the sight,
Their cry, and speed, renew.
The foremost ones, now reach his rear,
He turns, they dash away;
And circling now, the wrathful bear,
They have him full at bay.
At top of speed, the horse-men come,
All screaming in a row.
"Whoop! Take him Tiger. Seize him Drum."
Bang,—bang—the rifles go.
And furious now, the dogs he tears,
And crushes in his ire.
Wheels right and left, and upward rears,
With eyes of burning fire.
But leaden death is at his heart,
Vain all the strength he plies.
And, spouting blood from every part,
He reels, and sinks, and dies.
And now a dinsome clamor rose,
'Bout who should have his skin;
Who first draws blood, each hunter knows,
This prize must always win.
But who did this, and how to trace
What's true from what's a lie,
Like lawyers, in a murder case
They stoutly argufy.

Aforesaid fice, of blustering mood,
Behind, and quite forgot,
Just now emerging from the wood,
Arrives upon the spot.
With grinning teeth, and up-turned hair—
Brim full of spunk and wrath,
He growls, and seizes on dead bear,
And shakes for life and death.
And swells as if his skin would tear,
And growls and shakes again;
And swears, as plain as dog can swear,
That he has won the skin.
Conceited whelp! we laugh at thee—
Nor mind, that not a few
Of pompous, two-legged dogs there be,
Conceited quite as you.[15]

Letter to William H. Herndon, "My old withered dry eyes are full of tears yet."

Herndon, a young attorney whom Lincoln had mentored, became Lincoln's law partner in 1844. The speech that Lincoln refers to was given by Alexander H. Stephens, a Whig member of Congress from Georgia, condemning the Mexican-American War, which Lincoln also opposed.

Washington, February 2, 1848

Dear William:—I just take my pen to say that Mr. Stephens, of Georgia, a little, slim, pale-faced, consumptive man, with a voice like Logan's, has just concluded the very best speech of an hour's length I ever heard. My old withered dry eyes are full of tears yet.

If he writes it out anything like he delivered it, our people shall see a good many copies of it.[16]

Letter to Mary Todd Lincoln,
"In this troublesome world, we
are never quite satisfied."

Washington, April 16, 1848
Dear Mary:

In this troublesome world, we are never quite satisfied. When you were here, I thought you hindered me some in attending to business; but now, having nothing but business—no variety—it has grown exceedingly tasteless to me. I hate to sit down and direct documents, and I hate to stay in this old room by myself. You know I told you in last sunday's letter, I was going to make a little speech during the week; but the week has passed away without my getting a chance to do so; and now my interest in the subject has passed away too. Your second and third letters have been received since I wrote before. Dear Eddy thinks father is "gone tapila[.]" Has any further discovery been made as to the breaking into your grand-mother's house? If I were she, I would not remain there alone. You mention that your uncle John Parker is likely to be at Lexington. Dont forget to present him my very kindest regards.

I went yesterday to hunt the little plaid stockings, as you wished; but found that McKnight has quit business, and Allen had not a single pair of the description you give, and only one plaid pair of any sort that I thought would fit "Eddy's dear little feet." I have a notion to make another trial to-morrow morning. If I could get them, I have an excellent chance of sending them. Mr. Warrick Tunstall, of St. Louis is here. He is to leave early this week, and to go by Lexington. He says he knows you, and will call to see you; and he voluntarily asked, if I had not some package to send to you.

. . . Very soon after you went away, I got what I think a very pretty set of shirt-bosom studs—modest little ones, jet, set in gold, only costing 50 cents a piece, or 1.50 for the whole.

Mary Todd Lincoln, ca. 1846, in a daguerreotype taken by
the Springfield photographer Nicholas Shepherd.

Suppose you do not prefix the "Hon" to the address on your letters to me any more. I like the letters very much, but I would rather they should not have that upon them. It is not necessary, as I suppose you have thought, to have them to come free.

And you are entirely free from head-ache? That is good—good—considering it is the first spring you have been free from it since we were acquainted. I am afraid you will get so well, and fat, and young, as to be wanting to marry again. Tell Louisa I want her to watch you a little for me. Get weighed, and write me how much you weigh.[17]

To Mary Todd Lincoln, *"Will you be a good girl in all things, if I consent?"*

Washington, June 12, 1848
My dear wife:

On my return from Philadelphia, yesterday, where, in my anxiety I had been led to attend the whig convention I found your last letter. I was so tired and sleepy, having ridden all night, that I could not answer it till to-day; and now I have to do so in the H.R. [House of Representatives]. The leading matter in your letter, is your wish to return to this side of the Mountains. Will you be a good girl in all things, if I consent? Then come along, and that as soon as possible. Having got the idea in my head, I shall be impatient till I see you. You will not have money enough to bring you; but I presume your uncle will supply you, and I will refund him here. By the way you do not mention whether you have received the fifty dollars I sent you. I do not much fear but that you got it; because the want of it would have induced you [to?] say something in relation to it. If your uncle is already at Lexington, you might induce him to start on earlier than the first of July; he could stay in Kentucky longer on his return, and so make up for lost time. Since I began this letter, the H.R. has passed a resolution for adjourning on the 17th. July, which probably will pass the Senate. I hope this letter will not be disagreeable to you; which, together with the circumstances under which I write, I hope will excuse me for not writing a longer one. Come on just as soon as you can. I want to see you, and our dear—dear boys very much. Every body here wants to see our dear Bobby.[18]

An engraving of the Springfield house of Ninian and Elizabeth Todd Edwards, where Lincoln and Mary Todd had met in 1839 and were married in 1842. Elizabeth Todd Edwards was Mary Todd's older sister. Her husband had served with Lincoln in the Illinois state legislature.

Letters sent jointly to Thomas Lincoln and John D. Johnston in reply to requests for money, "I doubt whether since I saw you, you have done a good whole day's work in any one day."

Thomas Lincoln was Lincoln's father, and John D. Johnston his stepbrother— the son of Sarah Bush Lincoln, Thomas Lincoln's second wife.

Washington, Decr. 24th, 1848

My dear father: Your letter of the 7th. was received night before last. I very cheerfully send you the twenty dollars, which sum you say is necessary to save your land from sale. It is singular that you should have forgotten a judgment against you; and it is more singular that the plaintiff should have let you forget it so long, particularly as I suppose you have always had property enough to satisfy a judgment of that amount. Before you pay it, it would be well to be sure you have not paid it; or, at least, that you can not prove you have paid it. Give my love to Mother, and all the connections.

Dear Johnston:

Your request for eighty dollars, I do not think it best, to comply with now. At the various times when I have helped you a little, you have said to me "We can get along very well now" but in a very short time I find you in the same difficulty again. Now this can only happen by some defect in your conduct. What that defect is I think I know. You are not lazy, and still you are an idler. I doubt whether since I saw you, you have done a good whole day's work in any one day. You do not very much dislike to work; and still you do not work much, merely because it does not seem to you that you could get much for it. This habit of uselessly wasting time, is the whole difficulty; and it is vastly important to you, and still more so to your children that you should break this habit. It is more important to them, because they have longer to live, and can keep out of an idle habit before they are in it; easier than they can get out after they are in.

You are now in need of some ready money; and what I propose is, that you shall go to work, "tooth and nails" for some body who will give you money [for] it. Let father and your boys take charge of things at home—prepare for a crop, and make the crop; and you go to work for the best money wages, or in discharge of any debt you owe, that you can get. And to secure you a fair reward for your labor, I now promise you, that for every dollar you will, between this and the first of next May, get for your own labor, either in money, or in your own indebtedness, I will then give you one other dollar. By this, if you hire yourself at ten dolla[rs] a month, from me you will get ten more, making twenty dollars a month for your work. In this, I do not mean you shall go off to St. Louis, or the lead mines, or the gold mines, in Calif[ornia,] but I [mean for you to go at it for the best wages you] can get close to home [in] Coles county. Now if you will do this, you will soon be out of debt, and what is better, you will have a habit that will keep you from getting in debt again. But if I should now clear you out, next year you will be just as deep in as ever. You say you would almost give your place in Heaven for $70 or $80. Then you value your place in Heaven very

Thomas Lincoln (1779–1851), Abraham's father, in a photograph taken around 1840.

cheaply for I am sure you can with the offer I make you get the seventy or eighty dollars for four or five months work. You say if I furnish you the money you will deed me the land, and, if you dont pay the money back, you will deliver possession. Nonsense! If you cant now live with the land, how will you then live without it? You have always been [kind] to me, and I do not now mean to be unkind to you. On the contrary, if you will but follow my advice, you will find it worth more than eight times eighty dollars to you.[19]

Request for a Patent (1849)

Lincoln's experience as a laborer on flatboats, transporting cargo via river from Illinois to cities as far away as New Orleans, led him to devise a system for navigating shoals, which he patented in 1849. Lincoln is the only U.S. president to hold a patent.

IMPROVED METHOD OF LIFTING VESSELS OVER SHOALS.
Application for Patent:

What I claim as my invention, and desire to secure by letters patent, is the combination of expansible buoyant chambers placed at the sides of a vessel with the main shaft or shafts by means of the sliding spars, which pass down through the buoyant chambers and are made fast to their bottoms and the series of ropes and pulleys or their equivalents in such a manner that by turning the main shaft or shafts in one direction the buoyant chambers will be forced downward into the water, and at the same time expanded and filled with air for buoying up the vessel by the displacement of water, and by turning the shafts in an opposite direction the buoyant chambers will be contracted into a small space and secured against injury.[20]

Abraham Lincoln's patent drawings for using a system of shafts, sliding spars, buoyant chambers, and ropes and pulleys for lifting vessels over shoals. Lincoln's patent, number 6,469, was issued on May 22, 1849.

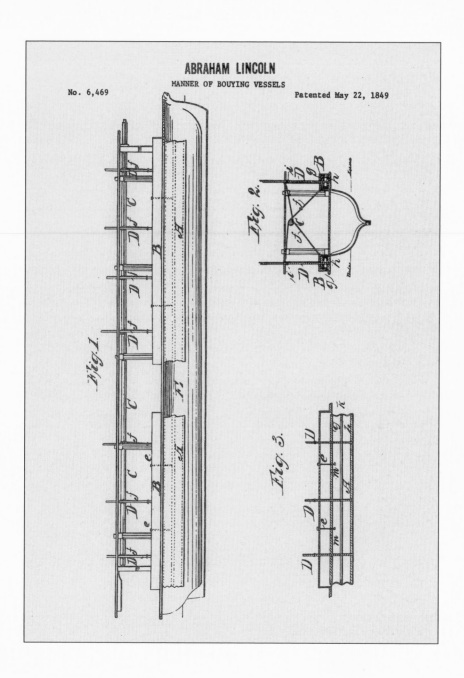

ABRAHAM LINCOLN

MANNER OF BOUYING VESSELS

No. 6,469

Patented May 22, 1849

To John M. Clayton,
"I respectfully decline the office."

Clayton, the Illinois secretary of state, had appointed Lincoln secretary of the Oregon Territory, to which Lincoln responded with this letter. Clayton later appointed him governor, a post Lincoln also refused.

Augt. 21st, 1849

Dear Sir: Your letter of the 10th. Inst., notifying me of my appointment as Secretary of the Teritory of Oregon, and accompanied by a Commission, has been duly received. I respectfully decline the office.

I shall be greatly obliged if the place be offered to Simeon Francis, of this place. He will accept it, is capable, and would be faithful in the discharge of it's duties. He is the principal editor of the oldest, and what I think may be fairly called, the leading Whig paper of the state,—the Illinois Journal. His good business habits are proved by the facts, that the paper has existed eighteen years, all the time weekly, and part of it, tri-weekly, and daily, and has not failed to issue regularly in a single instance.

Some time in May last, I think, Mr. Francis addressed a letter to Mr. Ewing, which, I was informed while at Washington in June, had been seen by the cabinet, and very highly approved. You possibly may remember it. He has, for a long time desired to go to Oregon; and I think his appointment would give general satisfaction[.][21]

Notes for a law lecture, "There is a vague popular belief that lawyers are necessarily dishonest."

[July 1, 1850?]

I am not an accomplished lawyer. I find quite as much material for a lecture in those points wherein I have failed, as in those wherein I have been moderately successful. The leading rule for the lawyer, as for the man of every other calling, is diligence. Leave nothing for to-morrow which can be done to-day. Never let your correspondence fall behind.

. . . Extemporaneous speaking should be practised and cultivated. It is the lawyer's avenue to the public. However able and faithful he may be in other respects, people are slow to bring him business if he cannot make a speech. And yet there is not a more fatal error to young lawyers than relying too much on speech-making. If any one, upon his rare powers of speaking, shall claim an exemption from the drudgery of the law, his case is a failure in advance.

Discourage litigation. Persuade your neighbors to compromise whenever you can. Point out to them how the nominal winner is often a real loser—in fees, expenses, and waste of time. As a peacemaker the lawyer has a superior opportunity of being a good man. There will still be business enough.

Never stir up litigation. A worse man can scarcely be found than one who does this. Who can be more nearly a fiend than he who habitually overhauls the register of deeds in search of defects in titles, whereon to stir up strife, and put money in his pocket? A moral tone ought to be infused into the profession which should drive such men out of it.

The matter of fees is important, far beyond the mere question of bread and butter involved. Properly attended to, fuller justice is done to both lawyer and client. An exorbitant fee should never be claimed. As a general rule never take your whole fee in advance, nor any more than a small retainer. When fully paid beforehand, you are more than a common mortal if you can feel the same interest in the case, as if something was still in prospect for you, as well as for your client. And when you lack interest in the case the job will very likely lack skill and diligence in the performance. Settle the amount of fee and take a note in advance. Then you will feel that you are working for something, and you are sure to do your work faithfully and well.

. . . There is a vague popular belief that lawyers are necessarily dishonest. I say vague, because when we consider to what extent confidence and honors are reposed in and conferred upon lawyers by the people, it appears improbable that their impression of dishonesty is very distinct and vivid. Yet the impression is common, almost universal. Let no young man choosing the law for a calling for a moment yield to the popular belief—resolve to be honest at all events; and if in your own judgment you cannot be an honest lawyer, resolve to be honest without being a lawyer. Choose some other occupation, rather than one in the choosing of which you do, in advance, consent to be a knave.[22]

Letter to John D. Johnston,
"Say to him that if we could meet now it is doubtful whether it would not be more painful than pleasant . . ."

In a letter to his stepbrother, Lincoln refuses a request to visit his dying father.

January 12, 1851

Dear brother:—On the day before yesterday I received a letter from Harriet [daughter of Dennis Hanks and Lincoln's stepsister, Elizabeth Johnston Hanks], written at Greenup. She says she has just returned from your house, and that father is very low and will hardly recover. She also says you have written me two letters, and that, although you do not expect me to come now, you wonder that I do not write.

I received both your letters, and although I have not answered them it is not because I have forgotten them, or been uninterested about them, but because it appeared to me that I could write nothing which would do any good. You already know I desire that neither father nor mother shall be in want of any comfort, either in health or sickness, while they live; and I feel sure you have not failed to use my name, if necessary, to procure a doctor, or anything else for father in his present sickness. My business is such that I could hardly leave home now, if it was not as it is, that my own wife is sick abed. (It is a case of baby-sickness, and I suppose is not dangerous.) I sincerely hope father may recover his health, but at all events, tell him to remember to call upon and confide in our great and good and merciful Maker, who will not turn away from him in any extremity. He notes the fall of a sparrow, and numbers the hairs of our heads, and He will not forget the dying man who puts his trust in Him. Say to him that if we could meet now it is doubtful whether it would not be more painful than pleasant, but that if it be his lot to go now, he will soon have a joyous meeting with many loved ones gone before, and where the rest of us, through the help of God, hope ere long to join them.

Write to me again when you receive this.[23]

To Andrew McCallen, a law client, "Vere ish my hundred tollars[?]"

Lincoln affects a German accent in his facetious demand for legal payment from a client after winning a case.

Springfield, Ills., July 4, 1851.
Dear Sir:

I have news from Ottawa, that we win our Galatin & Saline county case. As the dutch Justice said, when he married folks "Now, vere ish my hundred tollars"[24]

2. "As Opposite as God and Mammon"

Portrait of Abraham Lincoln as he looked in June 1860.

Congressional passage of the Kansas-Nebraska Act on May 22, 1854, injected new life into Lincoln's dormant political aspirations. Lincoln had been careful not to publicly oppose the Fugitive Slave Law (1850), which required free-state citizens and law enforcement to aid in the return of escaped slaves. Abolitionists and "radical" Republicans reviled the law, but Lincoln saw opposition to it as political suicide for himself and for the party. The Kansas-Nebraska Act, by contrast, effectively reversed the Missouri Compromise (1820), which had forbidden the expansion of slavery into the territory north of the 36°30' parallel. Now Lincoln saw clearly that slave owners were not content to continue the practice only where slavery was already established in law—they wanted the institution to expand west, where there were new economic opportunities and, not insignificantly, new bases of political power. Here he saw he could draw a moral and pragmatic line in the sand that might be politically viable. The man who would emerge as Lincoln's chief political antagonist, Stephen A. Douglas, author of the Kansas-Nebraska Act, effectively served as a foil for Lincoln's carefully constructed arguments against slavery and its expansion. This led directly to Lincoln's political rise.

Long an opponent of slavery in private, Lincoln now began to take a very public position on the issue in which he sought not only to demonstrate the moral bankruptcy of slavery, but also to illustrate its deleterious effects on the body politic. He pointed to what he believed was the hypocrisy of men like Douglas, who hid behind the smokescreen of "popular sovereignty," showing

An impassioned condemnation of the Fugitive Slave Act, passed by Congress in September 1850, which increased federal and free-state responsibility for the recovery of fugitive slaves.

with simple clarity the process by which slavery can become accepted and take root even in communities where slave holders are a small minority (Speech at Kalamazoo, p. 56).

In his 1854 Speech at Peoria (p. 50), he examines the words and actions of the founders, including the beloved Jefferson, showing their explicit intent and implicit wish for slavery to wither away. Jefferson, in particular, Lincoln argued, believed the literal truth that "all men are created equal," reminding Douglas and his supporters that Jefferson himself had warned that he "trembled for his country when he remembered that God was just" (p. 56). It is fascinating to read as Lincoln hones these positions, sharpening his speaking and debating skills in the mid-1850s, and then brilliantly deploys them in the famed Lincoln-Douglas debates of 1858. The debates themselves (pp. 72–73) are rightly regarded as a high point in American political discourse, and it's difficult to imagine a politician being more on his game than Lincoln was while vying with Douglas.

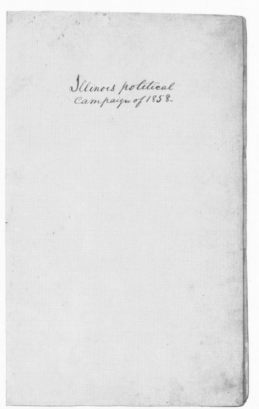

Illinois political
Campaign of 1858-

Lincoln himself kept a scrapbook of the newspaper coverage of the debates (which reported the speeches verbatim), hand-annotated them, and published them in book form in 1860.

Lincoln joined in the founding of the Illinois Republican party in 1856, immediately gaining the attention of the party's leadership when he delivered an inspiring oration that became known as the "Lost Speech," because those present failed to record it.

First page from a scrapbook of newspaper articles assembled by Abraham Lincoln during his campaign for U.S. Senate in 1858. See pages 70, 71, and 77 for interior pages from this scrapbook.

The essential ideas of that address, however, undoubtedly survive in Lincoln's many other speeches, written work, and notes to himself from that era. He spent much of 1856 stumping for the Republican presidential candidate, John C. Frémont, whose emancipation order as a Union general in Missouri Lincoln would later decide to reverse, at significant political cost.

Lincoln's personal correspondence from the era reveals greater personal depth and nuance in his thinking. For example, in his 1855 letter to his friend Joshua Speed, who was a slave holder, he said his antipathy toward slavery arose in part from the sight of shackled slaves during their "tedious" 1841 steamboat trip on the Ohio River, the memory of which had "continued [to] torment me." Lincoln goes on to gently chastise Speed for what he views as the deception behind popular sovereignty: "You say that if Kansas fairly votes herself a free State, as a Christian you will rejoice at it. All decent slaveholders talk that way, and I do not doubt their candor. But they never vote that way."

They also show Lincoln's political pragmatism—or, in the eyes of abolitionists and some contemporary critics, his lack of commitment to principle. He had been very careful to limit his opposition to slavery to what he considered politically feasible, namely the prevention of its expansion into the territories. Pressured in the months leading up to the presidential election of 1860 by the abolitionist wing of the Republican party to incorporate the repeal of the Fugitive Slave Law into the party platform, Lincoln demurred. He explained his reasoning to Salmon P. Chase, the abolitionist governor of Ohio (and Lincoln's future secretary of the treasury) in a June 1859 letter: "the introduction of a proposition for repeal of the Fugitive Slave law, into the next Republican National convention, will explode the convention and the party."[1]

Lincoln's run-up to the presidency is documented in letters between Lincoln and Republican political leaders. In one of them, Lincoln protests with typical humility, "I do not think myself fit for the presidency"; a few months later, after his successful speech at Cooper Union (p. 83), the ambitious autodidact from Illinois confessed to an ally, "The taste is in my mouth a little."

Lincoln delivered a heartfelt farewell speech to the people of Springfield before leaving on his journey by train to Washington, D.C., a journey that necessitated not only dozens of impromptu speeches but also subterfuge and even, infamously, disguise, because of threats to his life. But first, he sold off the totality of his home furnishings to a man named Samuel Melvin. His "windfall," per the itemized receipt (p. 96): $82.25.

Fragment on slavery, "By this rule, you are to be slave to the first man you meet, with an intellect superior to your own."

[April 1, 1854?]

If A. can prove, however conclusively, that he may, of right, enslave B.—why may not B. snatch the same argument, and prove equally, that he may enslave A?—

You say A. is white, and B. is black. It is color, then; the lighter, having the right to enslave the darker? Take care. By this rule, you are to be slave to the first man you meet, with a fairer skin than your own.

You do not mean color exactly?—You mean the whites are intellectually the superiors of the blacks, and, therefore have the right to enslave them? Take care again. By this rule, you are to be slave to the first man you meet, with an intellect superior to your own.

But, say you, it is a question of interest; and, if you can make it your interest, you have the right to enslave another. Very well. And if he can make it his interest, he has the right to enslave you.

To Jesse Lincoln, "there can be no doubt that you and I are of the same family."

Springfield, Illinois, April 1, 1854

My Dear Sir: On yesterday I had the pleasure of receiving your letter of the 16th of March. From what you say there can be no doubt that you and I are of the same family. The history of your family, as you give it, is precisely what I have always heard, and partly know, of my own. As you have supposed, I am the grandson of your uncle Abraham; and the story of his death by the Indians, and of Uncle Mordecai, then fourteen years old, killing one of the Indians, is the legend more strongly than all others imprinted upon my mind and memory. I am the son of grandfather's youngest son, Thomas. I have often heard my father speak of his uncle Isaac residing at Watauga (I think), near where the then States of Virginia, North Carolina, and Tennessee join,—you seem now to be some hundred miles or so west of that. I often saw Uncle Mordecai, and Uncle Josiah but once in my life; but I never resided near either of them. Uncle Mordecai died in 1831 or 2, in Hancock County, Illinois, where he had then recently removed from Kentucky, and where his children had also removed, and still reside, as I understand. Whether Uncle Josiah is dead or living, I cannot tell, not having heard from him for more than twenty years. When I last heard of [from] him he was living on Big Blue River, in Indiana (Harrison Co., I think), and where he had resided ever since the beginning of my recollection. My father (Thomas) died the 17th of January, 1851, in Coles County, Illinois, where he had resided twenty years. I am his only child. I have resided here, and here-abouts, twenty-three years. I am forty-five years of age, and have a wife and three children, the oldest eleven years. My wife was born and raised at Lexington, Kentucky; and my connection with her has some-times taken me there, where I have heard the older people of her relations speak of your uncle Thomas and his family. He is dead long ago, and his descendants have gone to some part of Missouri, as I recollect what I was told. When I was at Washington in 1848, I got up a correspondence with David Lincoln, residing at Sparta, Rockingham County, Virginia, who, like yourself, was a first cousin of my father; but I forget, if he informed me, which of my grandfather's brothers was his father. With Col. Crozier, of whom you speak, I formed quite an intimate acquaintance, for a short one, while at Washington; and when you meet him again I will thank you to present him my respects. Your present governor, Andrew Johnson, was also at Washington while I was; and he told me of there being people of the name of Lincoln in Carter County, I can no longer claim to be a young man myself; but I infer that, as you are of the same generation as my father, you are some older. I shall be very glad to hear from you again. Very truly your relative, A. LINCOLN.

Lincoln frequently made notes to himself, working out and refining ideas and phrases, throughout his political career. In this fragment, he broadly contemplates the purpose of government.

Fragment on government, "From this,
it appears that if all men were just,
there still would be some, though not
so much, need of government."

[July 1, 1854?]

The legitimate object of government, is to do for a community of people, whatever they need to have done, but can not do, at all, or can not, so well do, for themselves—in their separate, and individual capacities.

In all that the people can individually do as well for themselves, government ought not to interfere.

The desirable things which the individuals of a people can not do, or can not well do, for themselves, fall into two classes: those which have relation to wrongs, and those which have not. Each of these branch off into an infinite variety of subdivisions.

The first—that in relation to wrongs—embraces all crimes, misdemeanors, and non-performance of contracts. The other embraces all which, in its nature, and without wrong, requires combined action, as public roads and highways, public schools, charities, pauperism, orphanage, estates of the deceased, and the machinery of government itself.

From this it appears that if all men were just, there still would be some, though not so much, need of government.[2]

Speech at Peoria, Illinois, "by giving him the close, I felt confident you would stay for the fun of hearing him skin me."

Lincoln replies to his rival, U.S. Senator Stephen Douglas, jokingly telling the audience of his "selfish" reasons for giving Douglas the final word in the debate.

October 16, 1854

I do not rise to speak now, if I can stipulate with the audience to meet me here at half-past six or at seven o'clock. It is now several minutes past five, and Judge Douglas has spoken over three hours. If you hear me at all, I wish you to hear me through. It will take me as long as it has taken him. That will carry us beyond eight o'clock at night. Now, every one of you who can remain that long can just as well get his supper, meet me at seven, and remain an hour or two later. The Judge has already informed you that he is to have an hour to reply to me. I doubt not but you have been a little surprised to learn that I have consented to give one of his high reputation and known ability this advantage of me. Indeed, my consenting to it, though reluctant, was not wholly unselfish, for I suspected, if it were understood that the Judge was entirely done, you Democrats would leave and not hear me; but by giving him the close, I felt confident you would stay for the fun of hearing him skin me.[3]

From a speech given at Peoria, Illinois, on October 16, 1854, "I hate it because of the monstrous injustice of slavery itself."

Lincoln addresses a crowd on the recently enacted Kansas-Nebraska Act.

I think, and shall try to show, that it [the Kansas-Nebraska Act] is wrong— wrong in its direct effect, letting slavery into Kansas and Nebraska, and wrong in its prospective principle, allowing it to spread to every other part of the wide world where men can be found inclined to take it.

This declared indifference, but, as I must think, covert real zeal, for the spread of slavery, I cannot but hate. I hate it because of the monstrous injustice of slavery itself. I hate it because it deprives our republican example of its just influence in the world; enables the enemies of free institutions with plausibility to taunt us as hypocrites; causes the real friends of freedom to doubt our sincerity; and especially because it forces so many good men among ourselves into an open war with the very fundamental principles of civil liberty, criticizing the Declaration of Independence, and insisting that there is no right principle of action but self-interest.

. . . At the framing and adoption of the Constitution, [the founders] forbore to so much as mention the word "slave" or "slavery" in the whole instrument. In the provision for the recovery of fugitives, the slave is spoken of as a "person held to service or labor." In that prohibiting the abolition of the African slave trade for twenty years, that trade is spoken of as "the migration or importation of such persons as any of the States now existing shall think proper to admit," etc. These are the only provisions alluding to slavery. Thus the thing is hid away in the Constitution, just as an afflicted man hides away a wen or cancer which he dares not cut out at once, lest he bleed to death,—with the promise, nevertheless, that the cutting may begin at a certain time. Less than this our fathers could not do, and more they would not do. Necessity drove them so far, and farther they would not go. But this is not all. The earliest Congress under the Constitution took the same view of slavery. They hedged and hemmed it in to the narrowest limits of necessity.

In 1794 they prohibited an outgoing slave trade—that is, the taking of slaves from the United States to sell. In 1798 they prohibited the bringing of slaves from Africa into the Mississippi Territory, this Territory then comprising what are now the States of Mississippi and Alabama. This was ten years before they had the authority to do the same thing as to the States existing at the adoption of the Constitution. In 1800 they prohibited American citizens from trading in slaves between foreign countries, as, for instance, from Africa to Brazil. In 1803 they passed a law in aid of one or two slave-State laws in restraint of the internal slave trade. In 1807, in apparent hot haste, they passed the law, nearly a year in advance,—to take effect the first day of 1808, the very first day the Constitution would permit, prohibiting the African slave trade by heavy pecuniary and corporal penalties. In 1820, finding these provisions ineffectual, they declared the slave trade piracy, and annexed to it the extreme penalty of death. While all this was passing in the General Government, five or six of the original slave States had adopted systems of gradual emancipation, by which the institution was rapidly becoming extinct within their limits. Thus we see that the plain, unmistakable spirit of that age toward slavery was hostility to the principle and toleration only by necessity.

But now it is to be transformed into a "sacred right." Nebraska brings it forth, places it on the highroad to extension and perpetuity, and with a pat on its back says to it, "Go, and God speed you." Henceforth it is to be the chief jewel of the nation the very figure-head of the ship of state. Little by little, but steadily as man's march to the grave, we have been giving up the old for the new faith.

Near eighty years ago we began by declaring that all men are created equal; but now from that beginning we have run down to the other declaration, that for some men to enslave others is a "sacred right of self-government." These principles cannot stand together. They are as opposite as God and Mammon; and who ever holds to the one must despise the other.[4]

Reponse to Joshua Speed, "I am not a Know-Nothing; that is certain."

Lincoln's close friend Joshua Speed, like many Kentuckians, owned slaves.

Springfield, August 24, 1855

Dear Speed— . . . You suggest that in political action, now, you and I would differ. I suppose we would; not quite as much, however, as you may think. You know I dislike slavery, and you fully admit the abstract wrong of it. So far there is no cause of difference. But you say that sooner than yield your legal right to the slave, especially at the bidding of those who are not themselves interested, you would see the Union dissolved. I am not aware that any one is bidding you yield that right; very certainly I am not. I leave that matter entirely to yourself. I also acknowledge your rights and my obligations under the Constitution in regard to your slaves. I confess I hate to see the poor creatures hunted down and caught and carried back to their stripes and unrequited toil; but I bite my lips and keep quiet. In 1841 you and I had together a tedious low-water trip on a steamboat from Louisville to St. Louis. You may remember, as I well do, that from Louisville to the mouth of the Ohio there were on board ten or a dozen slaves shackled together with irons. That sight was a continued torment to me, and I see something like it every time I touch the Ohio or any other slave border. It is not fair for you to assume that I have no interest in a thing which has, and continually exercises, the power of making me miserable. You ought rather to appreciate how much the great body of the Northern people do crucify their feelings, in order to maintain their loyalty to the Constitution and the Union. I do oppose the extension of slavery because my judgment and feeling so prompt me, and I am under no obligations to the contrary. If for this you and I must differ, differ we must. You say, if you were President, you would send an army and hang the leaders of the Missouri outrages upon the Kansas elections; still, if Kansas fairly votes herself a slave State she must be admitted or the Union must be dissolved. But how if she votes herself a slave State unfairly, that is, by the very means for which you say you would hang men? Must she still be admitted, or the Union dissolved? That will be the phase of the question when it

Photograph of Lincoln taken in Chicago, Illinois, in 1854, during his campaign for the U.S. Senate.

first becomes a practical one. In your assumption that there may be a fair decision of the slavery question in Kansas, I plainly see you and I would differ about the Nebraska law. I look upon that enactment not as a law, but as a violence from the beginning. It was conceived in violence, is maintained in violence, and is being executed in violence. I say it was conceived in violence, because the destruction of the Missouri Compromise, under the circumstances, was nothing less than violence. It was passed in violence because it could not have passed at all but for the votes of many members in violence of the known will of their constituents. It is maintained in violence, because the elections since clearly demand its repeal; and the demand is openly disregarded.

You say men ought to be hung for the way they are executing the law; I say the way it is being executed is quite as good as any of its antecedents. It is being executed in the precise way which was intended from the first, else why does no Nebraska man express astonishment or condemnation? Poor Reeder [Andrew Reeder, the appointed governor of the Kansas territory] is the only public man who has been silly enough to believe that anything like fairness was ever intended, and he has been bravely undeceived.

That Kansas will form a slave constitution, and with it will ask to be admitted into the Union, I take to be already a settled question, and so settled by the very means you so pointedly condemn. By every principle of law ever held by any court North or South, every negro taken to Kansas is free; yet, in utter disregard of this,—in the spirit of violence merely,—that beautiful Legislature gravely passes a law to hang any man who shall venture to inform a negro of his legal rights. This is the subject and real object of the law. If, like Haman, they should hang upon the gallows of their own building, I shall not be among the mourners for their fate. In my humble sphere, I shall advocate the restoration of the Missouri Compromise so long as Kansas remains a Territory, and when, by all these foul means, it seeks to come into the Union as a slave State, I shall oppose it. I am very loath in any case to withhold my assent to the enjoyment of property acquired or located in good faith; but I do not admit that good faith in taking a negro to Kansas to be held in slavery is a probability with any man. Any man who has sense enough to be the controller of his own property has too much sense to misunderstand the outrageous character of the whole Nebraska business. But I digress. In my opposition to the admission of Kansas I shall have some company, but we may be beaten. If we are, I shall not on that account attempt to dissolve the Union. I think it probable, however, we shall be beaten. Standing as a unit among yourselves, You can, directly and indirectly, bribe enough of our men to carry the day, as you could on the open proposition to establish a monarchy.

Get hold of some man in the North whose position and ability is such that he can make the support of your measure, whatever it may be, a Democratic party necessity, and the thing is done. Apropos of this, let me tell you an anecdote. Douglas introduced the Nebraska Bill in January. In February afterward there was a called session of the Illinois Legislature. Of the one hundred members composing the two branches of that body, about seventy were Democrats. These latter held a caucus in which the Nebraska Bill was talked of, if not formally discussed. It was thereby discovered that just three, and no more, were in favor of the measure. In a day or two Douglas's orders came on to have resolutions passed approving the bill; and they were passed by large majorities!!!! The truth of this is vouched for by a bolting Democratic member. The masses, too, Democratic as well as Whig, were even nearer unanimous against it; but, as soon as the party necessity of supporting it became apparent, the way the Democrats began to see the wisdom and justice of it was perfectly astonishing.

You say that if Kansas fairly votes herself a free State, as a Christian you will rejoice at it. All decent slaveholders talk that way, and I do not doubt their candor. But they never vote that way. Although in a private letter or conversation you will express your preference that Kansas shall be free, you would vote for no man for Congress who would say the same thing publicly. No such man could be elected from any district in a slave State. You think Stringfellow [Andrew Stringfellow, a leader of the pro-slavery armed forces in Kansas] and company ought to be hung; and yet at the next Presidential election you will vote for the exact type and representative of Stringfellow. The slave-breeders and slave-traders are a small, odious, and detested class among you; and yet in politics they dictate the course of all of you, and are as completely your masters as you are the master of your own negroes. You inquire where I now stand. That is a disputed point. I think I am a Whig; but others say there are no Whigs, and that I am an Abolitionist. When I was at Washington, I voted for the Wilmot Proviso [a law proposed in 1846 to prohibit slavery in any territory gained from Mexico in the Mexican-American War, name for its congressional sponsor, David Wilmot] as good as forty times; and I never heard of any one attempting to un-Whig me for that. I now do no more than oppose the extension of slavery. I am not a Know-Nothing; that is certain. How could I be? How can any one who abhors the oppression of negroes be in favor of degrading classes of white people? Our progress in degeneracy appears to me to be pretty rapid. As a nation we began by declaring that "all men are created equal." We now practically read it "all men are created equal, except negroes." When the Know-Nothings get control, it will read "all men are created equal, except negroes and foreigners and Catholics." When it comes to this, I shall prefer emigrating to some country where they make no pretense of loving liberty,—to Russia, for instance, where despotism can be taken pure, and without the base alloy of hypocrisy.

Mary will probably pass a day or two in Louisville in October. My kindest regards to Mrs. Speed. On the leading subject of this letter I have more of her sympathy than I have of yours; and yet let me say I am,

Your friend forever,
A. LINCOLN.[5]

Excerpt of a speech delivered before the first Republican state convention of Illinois, held at Bloomington on May 29, 1856, "he trembled for his country when he remembered that God is just."

Thomas Jefferson, a slaveholder, mindful of the moral element in slavery, solemnly declared that he trembled for his country when he remembered that God is just; while Judge Douglas, with an insignificant wave of the hand, "don't care whether slavery is voted up or voted down." Now, if slavery is right, or even negative, he has a right to treat it in this trifling manner. But if it is a moral and political wrong, as all Christendom considers it to be, how can he answer to God for this attempt to spread and fortify it?[6]

Speech at Kalamazoo, Michigan, given August 27, 1856, "This is the way in which slavery is planted, and gains so firm a foothold."

. . . We will suppose that there are ten men who go into Kansas to settle. Nine of these are opposed to slavery. One has ten slaves. The slaveholder is a good man in other respects; he is a good neighbor, and being a wealthy man, he is enabled to do the others many neighborly kindnesses. They like the man, though they don't like the system by which he holds his fellow-men in bondage. And here let me say, that in intellectual and physical structure, our Southern brethren do not differ from us. They are, like us, subject to passions, and it is only their odious institution of slavery, that makes the breach between us. These ten men of whom I was speaking, live together three or four years; they intermarry; their family ties are strengthened. And who wonders that in time, the people learn to look upon slavery with complacency? This is the way in which slavery is planted, and gains so firm a foothold. I think this is a strong card that the Nebraska party have played, and won upon, in this game.[7]

Lincoln apparently liked this tousle-haired likeness of himself,
taken by the Chicago photographer Alexander Hesler in 1857.

Fragment of a speech at a Republican banquet in Chicago, December 10, 1856, "he might perceive that the 'rebuke' may not be quite as durable as he seems to think."

Lincoln chastens newly elected Democratic president James Buchanan, who had won an Electoral College majority, but only a modest plurality of the popular vote.

Like a rejected lover making merry at the wedding of his rival, the President felicitates himself hugely over the late Presidential election. He considers the result a signal triumph of good principles and good men, and a very pointed rebuke of bad ones. He says the people did it. He forgets that the "people," as he complacently calls only those who voted for Buchanan, are in a minority of the whole people by about four hundred thousand votes—one full tenth of all the votes. Remembering this, he might perceive that the "rebuke" may not be quite as durable as he seems to think—that the majority may not choose to remain permanently rebuked by that minority.[8]

Response to a speech by Stephen Douglas, "I protest against the counterfeit logic which concludes that, because I do not want a black woman for a slave I must necessarily want her for a wife."

Springfield, Illinois, June 26, 1857

There is a natural disgust in the minds of nearly all white people at the idea of an indiscriminate amalgamation of the white and black races; and Judge Douglas

Stephen A. Douglas (1813–1861), was in many respects the ideal political foil for Abraham Lincoln, in that the "Little Giant" was Lincoln's opposite: short (five feet, four inches), silver-tongued, educated, and proslavery. The debates between the two men in their races for U.S. Senate (1854 and 1858) and for president (1860) prompted the evolution of Lincoln's views and led directly to his rise to national prominence. After Lincoln's election in 1860, Douglas rallied to the cause of preserving the Union and became an important ally of the president's.

evidently is basing his chief hope upon the chances of his being able to appropriate the benefit of this disgust to himself. If he can, by much drumming and
repeating, fasten the odium of that idea upon his adversaries, he thinks he can
struggle through the storm. He therefore clings to this hope, as a drowning man
to the last plank. He makes an occasion for lugging it in from the opposition to
the Dred Scott decision. He finds the Republicans insisting that the Declaration of
Independence includes all men, black as well as white, and forthwith he boldly
denies that it includes negroes at all, and proceeds to argue gravely that all who
contend it does, do so only because they want to vote, and eat, and sleep, and
marry with negroes. He will have it that they cannot be consistent else. Now I
protest against the counterfeit logic which concludes that, because I do not want a
black woman for a slave I must necessarily want her for a wife. I need not have her
for either. I can just leave her alone. In some respects she certainly is not my equal;
but in her natural right to eat the bread she earns with her own hands, without
asking leave of any one else, she is my equal and the equal of all others.

. . . Chief Justice Taney, in his opinion in the Dred Scott case, admits that
the language of the Declaration is broad enough to include the whole human
family, but he and Judge Douglas argue that the authors of that instrument did
not intend to include negroes, by the fact that they did not at once actually place
them on an equality with the whites. Now this grave argument comes to just
nothing at all, by the other fact that they did not at once, or ever afterward,
actually place all white people on an equality with one another. And this is the
staple argument of both the Chief Justice and the Senator for doing this obvious
violence to the plain, unmistakable language of the Declaration.

I think the authors of that notable instrument intended to include all men,
but they did not intend to declare all men equal in all respects. They did not
mean to say all were equal in color, size, intellect, moral developments, or
social capacity. They defined with tolerable distinctness in what respects they
did consider all men created equal—equal with "certain inalienable rights,
among which are life, liberty, and the pursuit of happiness." This they said, and
this they meant.

. . . Now let us hear Judge Douglas's view of the same subject, as I find it in
the printed report of his late speech. Here it is:

"No man can vindicate the character, motives, and conduct of the signers of
the Declaration of Independence, except upon the hypothesis that they referred
to the white race alone, and not to the African, when they declared all men to
have been created equal; that they were speaking of British subjects on this

continent being equal to British subjects born and residing in Great Britain; that they were entitled to the same inalienable rights, and among them were enumerated life, liberty, and the pursuit of happiness. The Declaration was adopted for the purpose of justifying the colonists in the eyes of the civilized world in withdrawing their allegiance from the British crown, and dissolving their connection with the mother country."

My good friends, read that carefully over some leisure hour, and ponder well upon it; see what a mere wreck—mangled ruin—it makes of our once glorious Declaration.

"They were speaking of British subjects on this continent being equal to British subjects born and residing in Great Britain"! Why, according to this, not only negroes but white people outside of Great Britain and America were not spoken of in that instrument. The English, Irish, and Scotch, along with white Americans, were included, to be sure, but the French, Germans, and other white people of the world are all gone to pot along with the Judge's inferior races!

. . . Suppose, after you read it once in the old-fashioned way, you read it once more with Judge Douglas's version. It will then run thus:

"We hold these truths to be self-evident, that all British subjects who were on this continent eighty-one years ago were created equal to all British subjects born and then residing in Great Britain."

. . . But Judge Douglas is especially horrified at the thought of the mixing of blood by the white and black races. Agreed for once—a thousand times agreed. There are white men enough to marry all the white women and black men enough to marry all the black women; and so let them be married. On this point we fully agree with the Judge, and when he shall show that his policy is better adapted to prevent amalgamation than ours, we shall drop ours and adopt his. Let us see. In 1850 there were in the United States 405,751 mulattoes. Very few of these are the offspring of whites and free blacks; nearly all have sprung from black slaves and white masters. A separation of the races is the only perfect preventive of amalgamation; but as an immediate separation is impossible, the next best thing is to keep them apart where they are not already together. If white and black people never get together in Kansas, they will never mix blood in Kansas. That is at least one self-evident truth. A few free colored persons may get into the free States, in any event; but their number is too insignificant to amount to much in the way of mixing blood. In 1850 there were in the free States 56,649 mulattoes; but for the most part they were not born there—they came from the slave States, ready made up. In the same year the slave States had

348,874 mulattoes, all of home production. The proportion of free mulattoes to free blacks—the only colored classes in the free States is much greater in the slave than in the free States. It is worthy of note, too, that among the free States those which make the colored man the nearest equal to the white have proportionably the fewest mulattoes, the least of amalgamation. In New Hampshire, the State which goes farthest toward equality between the races, there are just

Lincoln's notes for the "A House Divided" speech, written around December 1857. Lincoln delivered the fully developed version of this speech as the opening address of his campaign for the U.S. Senate in 1858.

184 mulattoes, while there are in Virginia—how many do you think?—79,775, being 23,126 more than in all the free States together.

These statistics show that slavery is the greatest source of amalgamation, and next to it, not the elevation, but the degradation of the free blacks. Yet Judge Douglas dreads the slightest restraints on the spread of slavery, and the slightest human recognition of the negro, as tending horribly to amalgamation!

. . . I have said that the separation of the races is the only perfect preventive of amalgamation. I have no right to say all the members of the Republican party are in favor of this, nor to say that as a party they are in favor of it. There is nothing in their platform directly on the subject. But I can say a very large proportion of its members are for it, and that the chief plank in their platform— opposition to the spread of slavery—is most favorable to that separation.

Such separation, if ever effected at all, must be effected by colonization; and no political party, as such, is now doing anything directly for colonization. Party operations at present only favor or retard colonization incidentally. The enterprise is a difficult one; but "where there is a will there is a way," and what colonization needs most is a hearty will. Will springs from the two elements of moral sense and self-interest. Let us be brought to believe it is morally right, and at the same time favorable to, or at least not against, our interest to transfer the African to his native clime, and we shall find a way to do it, however great the task may be. The children of Israel, to such numbers as to include four hundred thousand fighting men, went out of Egyptian bondage in a body.[9]

Draft of speech—A House Divided, "I believe the government cannot endure permanently half slave and half free."

Ca. December 28, 1857

A house divided against itself cannot stand.

I believe the government cannot endure permanently half slave and half free. I expressed this belief a year ago; and subsequent developments have but confirmed me. I do not expect the Union to be dissolved. I do not expect the house to fall; but I do expect it will cease to be divided. It will become all one thing or all the other. Either the opponents of slavery will arrest the further spread of it, and put it in course of ultimate extinction; or its advocates will push it forward till it shall become alike lawful in all the States, old as well as new. Do you doubt it? Study the Dred Scott decision, and then see how little even now remains to be done. That decision may be reduced to three points.

The first is that a negro cannot be a citizen. That point is made in order to deprive the negro, in every possible event, of the benefit of that provision of the United States Constitution which declares that "the citizens of each State shall be entitled to all privileges and immunities of citizens in the several States."

The second point is that the United States Constitution protects slavery, as property, in all the United States territories, and that neither Congress, nor the people of the Territories, nor any other power, can prohibit it at any time prior to the formation of State constitutions.

This point is made in order that the Territories may safely be filled up with slaves, before the formation of State constitutions, thereby to embarrass the free-State sentiment, and enhance the chances of slave constitutions being adopted.

The third point decided is that the voluntary bringing of Dred Scott into Illinois by his master, and holding him here a long time as a slave, did not operate his emancipation—did not make him free.

This point is made, not to be pressed immediately; but if acquiesced in for a while, then to sustain the logical conclusion that what Dred Scott's master might lawfully do with Dred in the free State of Illinois, every other master may lawfully do with any other one or one hundred slaves in Illinois, or in any other free State. Auxiliary to all this, and working hand in hand with it, the Nebraska doctrine is to educate and mold public opinion to "not care whether slavery is voted up or voted down." At least Northern public opinion must cease to care anything about it. Southern public opinion may, without offense, continue to care as much as it pleases.

Welcome, or unwelcome, agreeable, or disagreeable, whether this shall be an entire slave nation, is the issue before us. Every incident—every little shifting of scenes or of actors—only clears away the intervening trash, compacts and consolidates the opposing hosts, and brings them more and more distinctly face to face.

The conflict will be a severe one; and it will be fought through by those who do care for the result, and not by those who do not care—by those who are for, and those who are against a legalized national slavery. The combined charge of Nebraskaism, and Dred Scottism must be repulsed, and rolled back. The deceitful cloak of "self-government" wherewith "the sum of all villanies" seeks to protect and adorn itself, must be torn from it's hateful carcass. That burlesque upon judicial decisions, and slander and profanation upon the honored names, and sacred history of republican America, must be overruled, and expunged from the books of authority.

To give the victory to the right, not bloody bullets, but peaceful ballots only, are necessary. Thanks to our good old constitution, and organization under it, these alone are necessary. It only needs that every right thinking man, shall go to the polls, and without fear or prejudice, vote as he thinks.[10]

Brief autobiography, "Education, defective."

Submitted by Lincoln to the compiler of the Dictionary of Congress *in 1858:*
June 15, 1858

Born February 12, 1809, in Hardin County, Kentucky.
Education, defective.
Profession, a lawyer.
Have been a captain of volunteers in Black Hawk war.
Postmaster at a very small office.
Four times a member of the Illinois Legislature and was a member of the lower house of Congress.[11]

Fragment on slavery, "We made the experiment; and the fruit is before us."

[April 1, 1854?]

Though Lincoln's secretaries Nicolas and Hay assigned this date to this fragment found after Lincoln's death, most scholars agree that it was most likely written for a speech given in 1857–1858.

The ant, who has toiled and dragged a crumb to his nest, will furiously defend the fruit of his labor, against whatever robber assails him. So plain, that the most dumb and stupid slave that ever toiled for a master, does constantly know that he is wronged. So plain that no one, high or low, ever does mistake it, except in a plainly selfish way; for although volume upon volume is written to prove slavery a very good thing, we never hear of the man who wishes to take the good of it, by being a slave himself.

Most governments have been based, practically, on the denial of equal rights of men, as I have, in part, stated them; ours began, by affirming those rights. They said, some men are too ignorant, and vicious, to share in government. Possibly so, said we; and, by your system, you would always keep them ignorant, and vicious. We proposed to give all a chance; and we expected the weak to grow stronger, the ignorant, wiser; and all better, and happier together.

We made the experiment; and the fruit is before us.[12]

Speech in Chicago, July 10, 1858, "I am not master of language; I have not a fine education . . ."

In this precursor to the "official debates," Lincoln replies to an earlier speech by Senator Douglas.

Judge Douglas thinks he discovers great political heresy. . . . He says I am in favor of making all the States of this Union uniform in all their internal regulations; that in all their domestic concerns I am in favor of making them entirely uniform. . . . He says that I am in favor of making war by the North upon the South for the extinction of slavery; that I am also in favor of inviting (as he expresses it) the South to a war upon the North for the purpose of nationalizing slavery. Now, it is singular enough, if you will carefully read that passage over, that I did not say that I was in favor of anything in it. I only said what I expected would take place. I made a prediction only,—it may have been a foolish one, perhaps. I did not even say that I desired that slavery should be put in course of ultimate extinction. I do say so now, however, so there need be no longer any difficulty about that. It may be written down in the great speech.

Gentlemen, Judge Douglas informed you that this speech of mine was probably carefully prepared. I admit that it was. I am not master of language; I have not a fine education; I am not capable of entering into a disquisition upon dialectics, as I believe you call it; but I do not believe the language I employed bears any such construction as Judge Douglas puts upon it. But I don't care about a quibble in regard to words. I know what I meant, and I will not leave this crowd in doubt, if I can explain it to them, what I really meant in the use of that paragraph.

I am not, in the first place, unaware that this government has endured eighty-two years half slave and half free. I know that. I am tolerably well acquainted with the history of the country, and I know that it has endured eighty-two years half slave and half free. I believe—and that is what I meant to allude to there—I believe it has endured because during all that time, until the introduction of the Nebraska Bill, the public mind did rest all the time in the belief that slavery was in course of ultimate extinction. That was what gave us the rest that we had through that period of eighty-two years,—at least, so I believe. I have always hated slavery, I think, as much as any Abolitionist,—I have been an Old Line Whig,—I have always hated it; but I have always been quiet about it until this new era of the introduction of the Nebraska Bill began. I always believed that everybody was against it, and that it was in course of ultimate extinction. [Pointing to Orville Browning, a political ally and close friend of Lincoln's who stood nearby.] Browning thought so; the great mass of the nation have rested in the belief that slavery was in course of ultimate extinction. They had reason so to believe.

The adoption of the Constitution and its attendant history led the people to believe so; and that such was the belief of the framers of the Constitution itself, why did those old men, about the time of the adoption of the Constitution, decree that slavery should not go into the new Territory, where it had not already gone? Why declare that within twenty years the African slave trade, by which slaves are supplied, might be cut off by Congress? Why were all these acts? I might enumerate more of these acts; but enough. What were they but a clear indication that the framers of the Constitution intended and expected the ultimate extinction of that institution? And now, when I say, as I said in my speech that Judge Douglas has quoted from, when I say that I think the opponents of slavery will resist the farther spread of it, and place it where the public mind shall rest with the belief that it is in course of ultimate extinction, I only mean to say that they will place it where the founders of this government originally placed it.

. . . We hold this annual [July Fourth] celebration to remind ourselves of all the good done in this process of time, of how it was done and who did it, and how we are historically connected with it; and we go from these meetings in better humor with ourselves, we feel more attached the one to the other, and more firmly bound to the country we inhabit. In every way we are better men in the age and race and country in which we live, for these celebrations. But after we have done all this we have not yet reached the whole. There is something else connected with it. We have—besides these, men descended by blood from our ancestors—among us perhaps half our people who are not descendants at all of these men; they are men who have come from Europe—German, Irish, French, and Scandinavian—men that have come from Europe themselves, or whose ancestors have come hither and settled here, finding themselves our equals in all things. If they look back through this history to trace their connection with those days by blood, they find they have none, they cannot carry themselves back into that glorious epoch and make themselves feel that they are part of us; but when they look through that old Declaration of Independence, they find that those old men say that "We hold these truths to be self-evident, that all men are created equal"; and then they feel that that moral sentiment, taught in that day, evidences their relation to those men, that it is the father of all moral principle in them, and that they have a right to claim it as though they were blood of the blood, and flesh of the flesh, of the men who wrote that Declaration; and so they are. That is the electric cord in that Declaration that links the hearts of patriotic and liberty-loving men together, that will link those patriotic hearts as long as the love of freedom exists in the minds of men throughout the world.

. . . Those arguments that are made, that the inferior race are to be treated with as much allowance as they are capable of enjoying; that as much is to be done for them as their condition will allow,—what are these arguments? They are the arguments that kings have made for enslaving the people in all ages of the world. You will find that all the arguments in favor of kingcraft were of this class; they always bestrode the necks of the people not that they wanted to do it, but because the people were better off for being ridden. That is their argument, and this argument of the Judge is the same old serpent that says, You work, and I eat; you toil, and I will enjoy the fruits of it. Turn in whatever way you will, whether it come from the mouth of a king, an excuse for enslaving the people of his country, or from the mouth of men of one race as a reason for enslaving the men of another race, it is all the same old serpent; and I hold, if that course of argumentation that is made for the purpose of convincing the public mind that we should not care about this should be granted, it does not stop with the negro. I should like to know, if taking this old Declaration of Independence, which declares that all men are equal upon principle, and making exceptions to it, where will it stop? If one man says it does not mean a negro, why not another say it does not mean some other man? If that Declaration is not the truth, let us get the statute book, in which we find it, and tear it out! Who is so bold as to do it? If it is not true, let us tear it out! [Cries of "No, no."] Let us stick to it, then; let us stand firmly by it, then.[13]

To Stephen A. Douglas, "none of the external circumstances have stood to my advantage."

Lincoln and Douglas negotiate the terms of their forthcoming debates.

Springfield, July 29, 1858
Dear Sir

Yours of the 24th. in relation to an arrangement to divide time and address the same audiences, is received; . . . Protesting that your insinuations of attempted unfairness on my part are unjust; and with the hope that you did not very considerately make them, I proceed to reply. To your statement that "It has been suggested recently that an arrangement had been made to bring out a third candidate for the U. S. Senate who, with yourself, should canvass the state in opposition to me &c." I can only say that such suggestion must have been made by yourself; for certainly none such has been made by, or to me; or otherwise, to my knowledge. Surely you did not deliberately conclude, as you insinuate, that I was expecting to draw you into an arrangement, of terms to be agreed on by yourself, by which a third candidate, and my self, "in concert, might be able to take the opening and closing speech in every case."

. . . For you to say that we have already spoken at Chicago and Springfield, and that on both occasions I had the concluding speech, is hardly a fair statement. The truth rather is this. At Chicago, July 9th, you made a carefully prepared conclusion on my speech of June 16th.; twentyfour hours after I made a hasty conclusion on yours of the 9th.; you had six days to prepare, and concluded on me again at Bloomington on the 16th.; twentyfour hours after I concluded on you again at Springfield. In the mean time you had made another conclusion on me at Springfield, which I did not hear, and of the contents of which I knew nothing when I spoke; so that your speech made in day-light, and mine at night of the 17th. at Springfield were both made in perfect independence of each other. The dates of making all these speeches, will show, I think, that in the matter of time for preparation, the advantage has all been on your side; and that none of the external circumstances have stood to my advantage.

I agree to an arrangement for us to speak at the seven places you have named, and at your own times, provided you name the times at once, so that I, as well as you, can have to myself the time not covered by the arrangement. As to other details, I wish perfect reciprocity, and no more. I wish as much time as you, and that conclusions shall alternate.

P.S. As matters now stand, I shall be at no more of your exclusive meetings; and for about a week from to-day a letter from you will reach me at Springfield. A. L.[14]

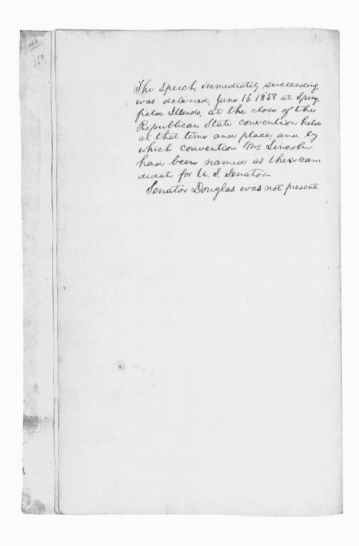

The speech, immediately succeeding, was delivered, June 16. 1858 at Spring field Illinois, at the close of the Republican State convention held at that time and place; and by which convention Mr Lincoln had been named as their candidate for U. S. Senator.

Senator Douglas was not present.

Above and left: Lincoln assembled a scrapbook of news clippings relating to the Lincoln-Douglas debates, which consisted primarily of transcripts of the speeches given by the candidates. Lincoln's handwritten annotations, in preparation for the publication of the speeches, can be seen on the pages. The book was published prior to the election of 1860, and quickly became a best seller. Douglas protested that Lincoln had revised and improved his own speeches without allowing Douglas the same opportunity.

From the first Lincoln-Douglas debate, Ottawa, Illinois, "I have no purpose, directly or indirectly, to interfere with the institution of slavery in the States where it exists."

August 21, 1858

I will say here, while upon this subject, that I have no purpose, directly or indirectly, to interfere with the institution of slavery in the States where it exists. I believe I have no lawful right to do so, and I have no inclination to do so. I have no purpose to introduce political and social equality between the white and the black races. There is a physical difference between the two which, in my judgment, will probably forever forbid their living together upon the footing of perfect equality; and inasmuch as it becomes a necessity that there must be a difference, I, as well as Judge Douglas, am in favor of the race to which I belong having the superior position. I have never said anything to the contrary, but I hold that, notwithstanding all this, there is no reason in the world why the negro is not entitled to all the natural rights enumerated in the Declaration of Independence, the right to life, liberty, and the pursuit of happiness. I hold that he is as much entitled to these as the white man. I agree with Judge Douglas he is not my equal in many respects, certainly not in color, perhaps not in moral or intellectual endowment. But in the right to eat the bread, without the leave of anybody else, which his own hand earns, he is my equal, and the equal of Judge Douglas, and the equal of every living man.

A painting that imagines the Lincoln-Douglas debate held in Charleston, Illinois, on September 18, 1858. Douglas sits at Lincoln's right.

From the fourth Lincoln-Douglas debate,
Charleston, Illinois, September 18, 1858,
"I tell him very frankly that I am not
in favor of negro citizenship."

Judge Douglas has said to you that he has not been able to get from me an answer to the question whether I am in favor of negro citizenship. So far as I know, the Judge never asked me the question before. [Applause.] He shall have no occasion to ever ask it again, for I tell him very frankly that I am not in favor of negro citizenship. [Renewed applause.] This furnishes me an occasion for saying a few words upon the subject. I mentioned in a certain speech of mine which has been printed, that the Supreme Court had decided that a negro could not possibly be made a citizen, and without saying what was my ground of complaint in regard to that, or whether I had any ground of complaint, Judge

Douglas has from that thing manufactured nearly every thing that he ever says about my disposition to produce an equality between the negroes and the white people. If any one will read my speech, he will find I mentioned that as one of the points decided in the course of the Supreme Court opinions, but I did not state what objection I had to it. But Judge Douglas tells the people what my objection was when I did not tell them myself. Now my opinion is that the different States have the power to make a negro a citizen under the Constitution of the United States if they choose. The Dred Scott decision decides that they have not that power. If the State of Illinois had that power I should be opposed to the exercise of it. [Cries of "good," "good," and applause.] That is all I have to say about it.[15]

Verses written to Rosa and Linnie Haggard in Rosa's autograph book (1858)

Lincoln had stayed in a hotel owned by their father in Winchester, Illinois, September 28, 1858.

To Rosa—

You are young, and I am older;
You are hopeful, I am not—
Enjoy life, ere it grow colder—
Pluck the roses ere they rot.
Teach your beau to heed the lay—
That sunshine soon is lost in shade—
That now's as good as any day—
To take thee, Rosa, ere she fade.

To Linnie—

A sweet plaintive song did I hear,
And I fancied that she was the singer—
May emotions as pure, as that song set a-stir
Be the worst that the future shall bring her.[16]

From the fifth Lincoln-Douglas debate, Galesburg, Illinois, "I will offer the highest premium in my power to Judge Douglas if he will show that he, in all his life, ever uttered a sentiment at all akin to that of Jefferson."

October 7, 1858

The Judge has alluded to the Declaration of Independence, and insisted that negroes are not included in that Declaration; and that it is a slander upon the framers of that instrument, to suppose that negroes were meant therein; and he asks you: Is it possible to believe that Mr. Jefferson, who penned the immortal paper, could have supposed himself applying the language of that instrument to the negro race, and yet held a portion of that race in slavery? Would he not at once have freed them? I only have to remark upon this part of the Judge's speech, (and that, too, very briefly, for I shall not detain myself, or you, upon that point for any great length of time,) that I believe the entire records of the world, from the date of the Declaration of Independence up to within three years ago, may be searched in vain for one single affirmation, from one single man, that the negro was not included in the Declaration of Independence. I think I may defy Judge Douglas to show that he ever said so, that Washington ever said so, that any President ever said so, that any member of Congress ever said so, or that any living man upon the whole earth ever said so, until the necessities of the present policy of the Democratic party, in regard to slavery, had to invent that affirmation. [Tremendous applause.] And I will remind Judge Douglas and this audience, that while Mr. Jefferson was the owner of slaves, as undoubtedly he was, in speaking upon this very subject, he used the strong language that "he trembled for his country when he remembered that God was just;" and I will offer the highest premium in my power to Judge Douglas if he will show that he, in all his life, ever uttered a sentiment at all akin to that of Jefferson. [Great applause and cries of "Hit him again," "good," "good."][17]

*From the seventh and final Lincoln-Douglas
debate, Alton, Illinois, "It is the eternal struggle
between these two principles—right and
wrong—throughout the world."*

October 15, 1858

... On this subject of treating it [slavery] as a wrong, and limiting its spread, let me say a word. Has any thing ever threatened the existence of this Union save and except this very institution of Slavery? What is it that we hold most dear amongst us? Our own liberty and prosperity. What has ever threatened our liberty and prosperity save and except this institution of Slavery? If this is true, how do you propose to improve the condition of things by enlarging Slavery— by spreading it out and making it bigger? You may have a wen or a cancer upon your person and not be able to cut it out lest you bleed to death; but surely it is no way to cure it, to engraft it and spread it over your whole body. That is no proper way of treating what you regard a wrong. You see this peaceful way of dealing with it as a wrong—restricting the spread of it, and not allowing it to go into new countries where it has not already existed. That is the peaceful way, the old-fashioned way, the way in which the fathers themselves set us the example.

... That is the real issue. That is the issue that will continue in this country when these poor tongues of Judge Douglas and myself shall be silent. It is the eternal struggle between these two principles—right and wrong—throughout the world. They are the two principles that have stood face to face from the beginning of time; and will ever continue to struggle. The one is the common right of humanity and the other the divine right of kings. It is the same principle in whatever shape it develops itself. It is the same spirit that says, "You work and toil and earn bread, and I'll eat it." [Loud applause.] No matter in what shape it comes, whether from the mouth of a king who seeks to bestride the people of his own nation and live by the fruit of their labor, or from one race of men as an apology for enslaving another race, it is the same tyrannical principle. I was glad to express my gratitude at Quincy, and I reexpress it here to Judge Douglas—that he looks to no end of the institution of slavery. That will help the people to see where the struggle really is. It will hereafter place with us all men who really do wish the wrong may have an end. And whenever we can get rid of the fog which obscures the real question—when we can get Judge Douglas and his friends to avow a policy looking to its perpetuation—we can get out

SPEECH OF

HON. ABRAHAM LINCOLN,

DELIVERED IN SPRINGFIELD, SATURDAY EVENING, JULY 17, 1858.

FELLOW CITIZENS:—Another election, which is deemed an important one, is approaching, and, as I suppose, the Republican party will, without much difficulty elect their State ticket. But in regard to the Legislature, we, the Republicans, labor under some disadvantages. In the first place, we have a Legislature to elect upon an apportionment of the representation made several years ago, when the proportion of the population was far greater in the South (as compared with the North) than it now is; and inasmuch as our opponents hold almost entire sway in the South, and we a correspondingly large majority in the North, the fact that we are now to be represented as we were years ago, when the population was different, is to us a very great disadvantage. We had, in the year 1855 according to law, a census or enumeration of the inhabitants, taken for the purpose of a new apportionment of representation. We know what a fair apportionment of representation upon that census would give us. We know that it could not if fairly made, fail to give the Republican party from six to ten more members of the Legislature than they can probably get as the law now stands. It so happened at the last session of the Legislature, that our opponents, holding the control of both branches of the Legislature, steadily refused to give us such an apportionment as we were rightly entitled to has upon the census already taken. The Legislature steadily refused to give us such an apportionment as we were rightfully entitled to have upon the census taken of the population of the State. The Legislature would pass no bill upon that subject, except such as we at least as unfair to us as the old one, and in which, in some instances, two men in the Democratic regions were allowed to go as far towards sending a member to the Legislature as three were in the Republican regions. Comparison was made at the time as to representative and senatorial districts, which completely demonstrated that such was the fact. Such a bill was passed, and tendered to the Republican Governor for his signature; but principally for the reasons I have stated, he withheld his approval, and the bill fell without becoming a law.

Another disadvantage under which we labor is, that there are one or two Democratic Senators who will be members of the next Legislature, and will vote for the election of Senator, who are holding over in districts in which we could, on all reasonable calculation, elect men of our own, if we only had the chance of an election. When we consider that there are but twenty five Senators in the Senate, taking two from the side where they rightfully belong and adding them to the other, is to us a disadvantage not to be lightly regarded. Still, so it is; we have this to contend with. Perhaps there is no ground of complaint on our part. In attending to the many things involved in the last general election for President, Governor, Auditor, Treasurer, Superintendent of Public Instruction, Members of Congress, of the Legislature, County officers, and so on, we allowed these things to happen by want of sufficient attention, and we have no cause to complain of our adversaries, so far as this matter is concerned. But we have some cause to complain of the refusal to give us a fair apportionment.

There is still another disadvantage under which we labor, and to which I will ask your attention. It arises out of the relative positions of the two persons who stand before the State as candidates for the Senate. Senator Douglas is of world wide renown. All the anxious politicians of his party, or who have been of his party for years past, have been looking upon him as certainly, at no distant day, to be the President of the United States. They have seen in his round jolly fruitful face, post-offices, land-offices, marshal-ships and cabinet appointments, chargeships and foreign missions, bursting and sprouting out in wonderful exuberance ready to be laid hold of by their greedy hands. [Great laughter.] And as they have been gazing upon this attractive picture so long, they cannot, in the little distraction that has taken place in the party, bring themselves to give up the charming hope; but with greedier anxiety they rush about him, sustain him, and give him marches, triumphal entries, and receptions beyond what even in the days of his highest prosperity they could have brought about in his favor. On the contrary nobody has ever expected me to be President. In my poor, lean, lank, face, nobody has ever seen that any cabbages were sprouting out. [Tremendous cheering and laughter.] These are disadvantages all, taken together, that the Republicans labor under. We have to fight this battle upon principle, and upon principle alone. I am, in a certain sense, made the standard-bearer in behalf of the Republicans. I was made so merely because there had to be some one so placed—I being in no wise, preferable to any other one of the twenty-five—perhaps a hundred we have in the Republican ranks. Then I say I wish it to be distinctly understood and borne in mind, that we have to fight this battle without many—perhaps without any—of the external aids which are brought to bear against us. So I hope those with whom I am surrounded have principle enough to nerve themselves for the task, and leave nothing undone, that can be fairly done, to bring about the right result.

After Senator Douglas left Washington, as his movements were made know by the public prints, he tarried a considerable time in the city of New York and it was heralded that, like another Napoleon, he was lying by, and framing the plan of his campaign. It was telegraphed to Washington City, and published in the Union that he was framing his plan for the purpose of going to Illinois to pounce upon and annihilate the treasonable and disunion speech which Lincoln had made here on the 16th of June. Now, I do suppose that the Judge really spent some time in New York maturing the plan of the campaign, as his friends heralded for him. I have been able, by noting his movements since his arrival in Illinois, to discover evidences confirmatory of that allegation. I think I have been able to see what are the material points of that plan. I will for a little while, ask your attention to some of them. What I shall point out, though not showing the whole plan are nevertheless the main points, I suppose.

They are not very numerous. The first is Popular Sovereignty. The second and third are attacks upon my speech made on the 16th of June. Out of these three points—drawing within the range of Popular Sovereignty the question of the Lecompton Constitution—he makes his principal assault. Upon these his successive speeches are substantially one and the same. On this matter of Popular Sovereignty I wish to be a little careful. Auxiliary to these main points, to be sure, are their thunderings of cannon, their marching and music, their fizzlegigs and fireworks; but I will not waste time with them. They are but the little trappings of the campaign.

Coming to the substance—the first point—"Popular Sovereignty." It is to be labelled upon the cars in which he travels; put upon the hacks he rides in; to be flaunted upon the arches he passes under, and the banners which wave over him. It is to be dished up in as many varieties as a French cook can produce soups from potatoes. Now, as this is so great a staple of the plan of the campaign, it is worth while to examine it carefully; and if we examine only a very little, and do not allow ourselves to be misled, ye shall be able to see that the whole thing is the most arrant Quixotism that was ever enacted before a community. What is the matter of Popular Sovereignty? The first thing, in order to understand it, is to get a good definition of what it is, and after that to see how it is applied.

I suppose almost every one knows, that in this controversy, whatever has been said has had reference to the question of negro slavery. We have not been in a controversy about the right of the people to govern themselves in the ordinary matters of domestic concern in the States and Territories. Mr. Buchanan in one of his late messages, (I think when he sent up the Lecompton Constitution,) urged that the main points to which the public attention had been directed, was not in regard to the great variety of small domestic matters, but was directed to the question of negro slavery; and he assorted, that if the people had had a fair chance to vote on that question, there was no reasonable ground of objection in regard to minor questions. Now, while I think that the people had not had given, or offered them, a fair chance upon that slavery question; still, if there had been a fair submission to a vote upon that main question, the President's proposition

A page from the Lincoln-Douglas debate scrapbook, assembled by Abraham Lincoln (see caption on page 71 for details). In his notes to the printer, Lincoln deleted crowd reactions and made small clarifications to his own remarks.

from among them that class of men and bring them to the side of those who treat it as a wrong. Then there will soon be an end of it, and that end will be its "ultimate extinction." Whenever the issue can be distinctly made, and all extraneous matter thrown out so that men can fairly see the real difference between the parties, this controversy will soon be settled, and it will be done peaceably too. There will be no war, no violence. It will be placed again where the wisest and best men of the world, placed it. Brooks of South Carolina [Preston Brooks, a congressman famous for beating the abolitionist (and future Lincoln cabinet member) Senator Charles Sumner with a cane on the floor of the Senate in 1856], once declared that when this Constitution was framed, its framers did not look to the institution existing until this day. When he said this, I think he stated a fact that is fully borne out by the history of the times. But he also said they were better and wiser men than the men of these days; yet the men of these days had experience which they had not, and by the invention of the cotton gin it became a necessity in this country that slavery should be perpetual. I now say that willingly or unwillingly, purposely or without purpose, Judge Douglas has been the most prominent instrument in changing the position of the institution of slavery which the fathers of the government expected to come to an end ere this—and putting it upon Brooks' cotton gin basis, [Great applause,]—placing it where he openly confesses he has no desire there shall ever be an end of it. [Renewed applause.][18]

Letter to Henry L. Pierce and others, "they have performed the same feat as the two drunken men."

Lincoln on the ideological reversal on the subject of personal and property rights between Democrats and "the anti-Jefferson party."

April 6, 1859

Remembering . . . that the Jefferson party was formed upon its supposed superior devotion to the personal rights of men, holding the rights of property to be secondary only, and greatly inferior, and assuming that the so-called Democracy of to-day are the Jefferson, and their opponents the anti-Jefferson, party, it will be equally interesting to note how completely the two have changed hands as to the principle upon which they were originally supposed to be divided. The Democracy of to-day hold the liberty of one man to be absolutely nothing, when in conflict with another man's right of property; Republicans, on the contrary, are for both the man and the dollar, but in case of conflict the man before the dollar.

I remember being once much amused at seeing two partially intoxicated men engaged in a fight with their great-coats on, which fight, after a long and rather harmless contest, ended in each having fought himself out of his own coat and into that of the other. If the two leading parties of this day are really identical with the two in the days of Jefferson and Adams, they have performed the same feat as the two drunken men.[19]

Contract with Theodore Canisius, regarding the purchase of a printing press for a German-language, pro-Republican newspaper

May [30?] 1859

This instrument witnesseth that the Printing-press, german types &c. purchased of John Burkhardt, belong to Abraham Lincoln; that Theodore Canissius is to have immediate possession of them, and is to commence publishing in Springfield, Illinois, a Republican newspaper, to be chiefly in the german language, with occasional translations into English at his option; the first number to issue in the ensuing month of June, and to continue thenceforward issuing weekly or oftener, at the option of said Cannissius, he, said Cannissius, bearing all expences, and charges, and taking all incomes and profits; said paper, in political sentiment, not to depart from the Philadelphia and Illinois Republican platforms; and for a material departure in that respect, or a failure of said paper to issue as often as weekly, or any attempt to remove said press, types &c, from Springfield, or to print with them any thing opposed to, or designed to injure the Republican party, said Lincoln may, at his option, at once take possession of said press, types &c, and deal with them as his own. On the contrary, if said Canissius shall issue a newspaper, in all things conformable hereto, until after the Presidential election of 1860, then said press, types &c are to be his property absolutely, not, however, to be used against the Republican party; nor to be removed from Springfield without the consent of said Lincoln. A. LINCOLN

    May 1859 TH CANISIUS

    May 30, 1859. Jacob Bunn, bought the press, types &c. of John Burkhardt, for me, and with my money. A. LINCOLN[20]

Fragment from Lincoln's notes for a speech, written around September 1859

Negro equality! Fudge!! How long, in the government of a God, great enough to make and maintain this Universe, shall there continue knaves to vend, and fools to gulp, so low a piece of demagougeism as this.[21]

Lincoln's inscription in the autograph album of Mary Delahay, "With pleasure I write my name in your Album."

Mary Delahay was the daughter of Lincoln's good friend Mark Delahay, an attorney then living in Kansas. Lincoln appointed him to the federal bench in 1863.

December 7, 1859
Dear Mary

With pleasure I write my name in your Album. Ere long some younger man will be more happy to confer his name upon you.

    Dont allow it, Mary, until fully assured that he is worthy of the happiness. Dec. 7, 1859. Your friend, A. LINCOLN[22]

Letter to Samuel Galloway, "I must say I do not think myself fit for the Presidency."

Galloway was a Columbus, Ohio–based attorney and a member of the U.S. House of Representatives. He led the group that approached Lincoln for the first time about a possible nomination to become the Republican candidate for president in 1860.

Springfield, Ill., July 28, 1859

My dear Sir:—Your very complimentary, not to say flattering, letter of the 23d inst. is received. Dr. Reynolds [the president of Illinois University and pastor of the English Lutheran Church at Springfield, and a Lincoln supporter] had induced me to expect you here; and I was disappointed not a little by your failure to come. And yet I fear you have formed an estimate of me which can scarcely be sustained on a personal acquaintance.

   . . . I must say I do not think myself fit for the Presidency.[23]

Lincoln's response to a request for an autobiographical sketch from Jesse W. Fell, for publication in a Pennsylvania newspaper, " 'readin', writin', and cipherin' ' to the Rule of Three."

The biography was picked up widely by other newspapers.

Springfield, December 20, 1859

My dear Sir:—Herewith is a little sketch, as you requested. There is not much of it, for the reason, I suppose, that there is not much of me. If anything be made out of it, I wish it to be modest, and not to go beyond the material. If it were thought necessary to incorporate anything from any of my speeches

I suppose there would be no objection. Of course it must not appear to have been written by myself.

Yours very truly, A. LINCOLN

———

I was born February 12, 1809, in Hardin County, Kentucky. My parents were both born in Virginia, of undistinguished families—second families, perhaps I should say. My mother, who died in my tenth year, was of a family of the name of Hanks, some of whom now reside in Adams, and others in Macon County, Illinois. My paternal grandfather, Abraham Lincoln, emigrated from Rockingham County, Virginia, to Kentucky about 1781 or 1782, where a year or two later he was killed by the Indians, not in battle, but by stealth, when he was laboring to open a farm in the forest. His ancestors, who were Quakers, went to Virginia from Berks County, Pennsylvania. An effort to identify them with the New England family of the same name ended in nothing more definite than a similarity of Christian names in both families, such as Enoch, Levi, Mordecai, Solomon, Abraham, and the like.

My father, at the death of his father, was but six years of age, and he grew up literally without education. He removed from Kentucky to what is now Spencer County, Indiana, in my eighth year. We reached our new home about the time that State came into the Union. It was a wild region, with many bears and other wild animals still in the woods. There I grew up. There were some schools, so called, but no qualification was ever required of a teacher beyond "readin', writin', and cipherin'" to the Rule of Three. If a straggler supposed to understand Latin happened to sojourn in the neighborhood he was looked upon as a wizard. There was absolutely nothing to excite ambition for education. Of course, when I came of age I did not know much. Still, somehow, I could read, write, and cipher to the Rule of Three, but that was all. I have not been to school since. The little advance I now have upon this store of education I have picked up from time to time under the pressure of necessity.

I was raised to farm work, which I continued till I was twenty-two. At twenty-one I came to Illinois, Macon County. Then I got to New Salem, at that time in Sangamon, now in Menard County, where I remained a year as a sort of clerk in a store. Then came the Black Hawk war; and I was elected a captain of volunteers, a success which gave me more pleasure than any I have had since. I went the campaign, was elected, ran for the Legislature the same year (1832), and was beaten—the only time I ever have been beaten by the people. The next and three succeeding biennial elections I was elected to the

Legislature. I was not a candidate afterward. During this legislative period I had studied law, and removed to Springfield to practice it. In 1846 I was once elected to the lower House of Congress. Was not a candidate for re-election. From 1849 to 1854, both inclusive, practiced law more assiduously than ever before. Always a Whig in politics; and generally on the Whig electoral tickets, making active canvasses. I was losing interest in politics when the repeal of the Missouri Compromise aroused me again. What I have done since then is pretty well known.

If any personal description of me is thought desirable, it may be said I am, in height, six feet four inches, nearly; lean in flesh, weighing on an average one hundred and eighty pounds; dark complexion, with coarse black hair and gray eyes. No other marks or brands recollected.[24]

Address at Cooper Union, New York City, "Let us have faith that right makes might. . ."

February 27, 1860

Mr. President and fellow-citizens of New-York:—The facts with which I shall deal this evening are mainly old and familiar; nor is there anything new in the general use I shall make of them. If there shall be any novelty, it will be in the mode of presenting the facts, and the inferences and observations following that presentation.

. . . And now, if they would listen—as I suppose they will not—I would address a few words to the Southern people.

I would say to them:—You consider yourselves a reasonable and a just people; and I consider that in the general qualities of reason and justice you are not inferior to any other people. Still, when you speak of us Republicans, you do so only to denounce us as reptiles, or, at the best, as no better than outlaws. You will grant a hearing to pirates or murderers, but nothing like it to "Black Republicans." In all your contentions with one another, each of you deems an unconditional condemnation of "Black Republicanism" as the first thing to be attended to. Indeed, such condemnation of us seems to be an indispensable prerequisite—license, so to speak—among you to be admitted or permitted to speak at all. Now, can you, or not, be prevailed upon to pause and to consider

whether this is quite just to us, or even to yourselves? Bring forward your charges and specifications, and then be patient long enough to hear us deny or justify.

You say we are sectional. We deny it. That makes an issue; and the burden of proof is upon you. You produce your proof; and what is it? Why, that our party has no existence in your section—gets no votes in your section. The fact is substantially true; but does it prove the issue? If it does, then in case we should, without change of principle, begin to get votes in your section, we should thereby cease to be sectional. You cannot escape this conclusion; and yet, are you willing to abide by it? If you are, you will probably soon find that we have ceased to be sectional, for we shall get votes in your section this very year. You will then begin to discover, as the truth plainly is, that your proof does not touch the issue. The fact that we get no votes in your section, is a fact of your making, and not of ours. And if there be fault in that fact, that fault is primarily yours, and remains so until you show that we repel you by some wrong principle or practice. If we do repel you by any wrong principle or practice, the fault is ours; but this brings you to where you ought to have started—to a discussion of the right or wrong of our principle. If our principle, put in practice, would wrong your section for the benefit of ours, or for any other object, then our principle, and we with it, are sectional, and are justly opposed and denounced as such. Meet us, then, on the question of whether our principle, put in practice, would wrong your section; and so meet us as if it were possible that something may be said on our side.

. . . But you will break up the Union rather than submit to a denial of your Constitutional rights.

That has a somewhat reckless sound; but it would be palliated, if not fully justified, were we proposing, by the mere force of numbers, to deprive you of some right, plainly written down in the Constitution. But we are proposing no such thing.

When you make these declarations, you have a specific and well-understood allusion to an assumed Constitutional right of yours, to take slaves into the federal territories, and to hold them there as property. But no such right is specifically written in the Constitution. That instrument is literally silent about

A rare standing portrait of Lincoln taken in the Mathew Brady studio in New York around the time of Lincoln's appearance at the Cooper Institute, as Cooper Union was then commonly called.

any such right. We, on the contrary, deny that such a right has any existence in the Constitution, even by implication.

Your purpose, then, plainly stated, is, that you will destroy the Government, unless you be allowed to construe and enforce the Constitution as you please, on all points in dispute between you and us. You will rule or ruin in all events.

Will they be satisfied if the Territories be unconditionally surrendered to them? We know they will not. In all their present complaints against us, the Territories are scarcely mentioned. Invasions and insurrections are the rage now. Will it satisfy them, if, in the future, we have nothing to do with invasions and insurrections? We know it will not. We so know, because we know we never had anything to do with invasions and insurrections; and yet this total abstaining does not exempt us from the charge and the denunciation.

The question recurs, what will satisfy them? Simply this: We must not only let them alone, but we must, somehow, convince them that we do let them alone. This, we know by experience, is no easy task. We have been so trying to convince them from the very beginning of our organization, but with no success. In all our platforms and speeches we have constantly protested our purpose to let them alone; but this has had no tendency to convince them. Alike unavailing to convince them, is the fact that they have never detected a man of us in any attempt to disturb them.

These natural, and apparently adequate means all failing, what will convince them? This, and this only: cease to call slavery wrong, and join them in calling it right. And this must be done thoroughly—done in acts as well as in words. Silence will not be tolerated—we must place ourselves avowedly with them. Senator Douglas's new sedition law must be enacted and enforced, suppressing all declarations that slavery is wrong, whether made in politics, in presses, in pulpits, or in private. We must arrest and return their fugitive slaves with greedy pleasure. We must pull down our Free State constitutions. The whole atmosphere must be disinfected from all taint of opposition to slavery, before they will cease to believe that all their troubles proceed from us.

. . . Holding, as they do, that slavery is morally right, and socially elevating, they cannot cease to demand a full national recognition of it, as a legal right, and a social blessing.

Nor can we justifiably withhold this, on any ground save our conviction that slavery is wrong. If slavery is right, all words, acts, laws, and constitutions against it, are themselves wrong, and should be silenced, and swept away. If it is right, we cannot justly object to its nationality—its universality; if it is wrong, they cannot justly insist upon its extension—its enlargement. All they ask, we could readily grant, if we thought slavery right; all we ask, they could as readily grant, if they thought it wrong. Their thinking it right, and our thinking it wrong, is the precise fact upon which depends the whole controversy. Thinking it right, as they do, they are not to blame for desiring its full recognition, as being right; but, thinking it wrong, as we do, can we yield to them? Can we cast our votes with their view, and against our own? In view of our moral, social, and political responsibilities, can we do this?

Wrong as we think slavery is, we can yet afford to let it alone where it is, because that much is due to the necessity arising from its actual presence in the nation; but can we, while our votes will prevent it, allow it to spread into the National Territories, and to overrun us here in these Free States? If our sense of duty forbids this, then let us stand by our duty, fearlessly and effectively. Let us be diverted by none of those sophistical contrivances wherewith we are so industriously plied and belabored—contrivances such as groping for some middle ground between the right and the wrong, vain as the search for a man who should be neither a living man nor a dead man—such as a policy of "don't care" on a question about which all true men do care—such as Union appeals beseeching true Union men to yield to Disunionists, reversing the divine rule, and calling, not the sinners, but the righteous to repentance—such as invocations to Washington, imploring men to unsay what Washington said, and undo what Washington did.

Neither let us be slandered from our duty by false accusations against us, nor frightened from it by menaces of destruction to the Government nor of dungeons to ourselves. LET US HAVE FAITH THAT RIGHT MAKES MIGHT, AND IN THAT FAITH, LET US, TO THE END, DARE TO DO OUR DUTY AS WE UNDERSTAND IT.[25]

Notes for speech at Hartford, Connecticut (recovered by a reporter after Lincoln's speech there)

[March 5, 1860]

SIGNS OF DECAY—BUSHWHACKING—
IRREPRESSIBLE CONFLICT—
JOHN BROWN
SHOE-TRADE—
True, or not true.
If true, what?
Mason
Plasters.
If not true, what?
[Illegible] is the question.
We must deal with it.
Magnitude of question.
What prevents just now?
Right — wrong — indifference
Indifference unphilosophical
Because nobody is indifferent
Must be converted to
Can be, or can not be done.
I suppose can not.
But if can, what result?
Indifference, then, must be rejected.
And what supported?
Sectionalism
Conservatism
John Brown
Conclusion[26]

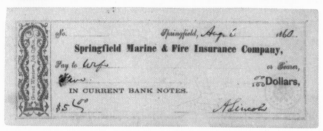

Lincoln's family business: Checks drawn on Lincoln's Springfield bank, reimbursing himself for expenses incurred during the run-up to his presidential campaign; and to Mary, presumably for her personal expenses during the same period. Lincoln attended a Republican rally in Springfield on the day he wrote this check.

Letter to Harvey G. Eastman in reply to a request for a photograph

Eastman was an abolitionist and Lincoln supporter from Poughkeepsie, New York. Lincoln is referring to the Mathew Brady portrait taken on February 27, 1860, prior to Lincoln's Cooper Union speech.

Springfield, Ills., April 7, 1860
Dear Sir

Yours of March 18th. addressed to me at Chicago, and requesting my photograph is received. I have not a single one now at my control; but I think you can easily get one at New-York. While I was there I was taken to one of the places where they get up such things, and I suppose they got my shaddow, and can multiply copies indefinitely. Any of the Republican Club men there can show you the place.[27]

Letter to Lyman Trumbull in response to an inquiry about the Republican presidential nomination, "The taste is in my mouth a little . . ."

Trumbull, a Republican senator from Illinois, was a supporter of Lincoln's. He later co-authored the Thirteenth Amendment to the Constitution abolishing slavery.

Springfield, April 29, 1860
My dear Sir:

. . . As you request, I will be entirely frank. The taste is in my mouth a little; and this, no doubt, disqualifies me, to some extent, to form correct opinions. You may confidently rely, however, that by no advice or consent of mine, shall my presentations be pressed to the point of endangering our common cause.

Recurring to Illinois, we want something here quite as much as, and which is harder to get than, the electoral vote—the Legislature. And it is exactly in this point that Seward's nomination would be hard upon us. Suppose he should gain us a thousand votes in Winnebago, it would not compensate for the loss of fifty in Edgar.

. . . A word now for your own special benefit. You better write no letters which can possibly be distorted into opposition, or quasi opposition to me. There are men on the constant watch for such things out of which to prejudice my peculiar friends against you. While I have no more suspicion of you than I have of my best friend living, I am kept in a constant struggle against suggestions of this sort. I have hesitated some to write this paragraph, lest you should suspect I do it for my own benefit, and not for yours; but on reflection I conclude you will not suspect me.

Let no eye but your own see this—not that there is anything wrong, or even ungenerous, in it; but it would be misconstrued.[28]

A Currier & Ives satirical cartoon from the 1860 election shows Lincoln contemplating which of his Democratic opponents to eat first.

Lincoln's reply to the 1860 Republican
presidential nominating committee when
they visited his home to inform him
officially of his selection as the Republican
presidential candidate in 1860

May 19, 1860

Mr. Chairman and gentlemen of the committee:—I tender to you, and through you to the Republican National Convention, and all the people represented in it, my profoundest thanks for the high honor done me, which you now formally announce. Deeply and even painfully sensible of the great responsibility which is inseparable from this high honor—a responsibility which I could almost wish had fallen upon some one of the far more eminent men and experienced statesmen whose distinguished names were before the

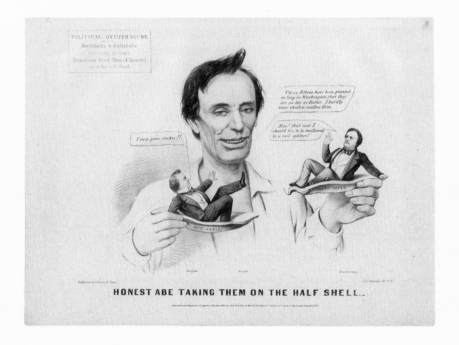

HONEST ABE TAKING THEM ON THE HALF SHELL..

convention—I shall, by your leave, consider more fully the resolutions of the convention, denominated their platform, and without any unnecessary or unreasonable delay respond to you, Mr. Chairman, in writing—not doubting that the platform will be found satisfactory, and the nomination gratefully accepted.

And now I will not longer defer the pleasure of taking you, and each of you, by the hand.[29]

Lincoln's letter to George Ashmun, the president of the Republican National Committee, accepting the nomination as the Republican candidate for president in 1860

May 23, 1860

Sir:—I accept the nomination tendered me by the convention over which you presided, and of which I am formally apprised in the letter of yourself and others, acting as a committee of the convention for that purpose.

The declaration of principles and sentiments which accompanies your letter meets my approval; and it shall be my care not to violate or disregard it in any part.

Imploring the assistance of Divine Providence, and with due regard to the views and feelings of all who were represented in the convention, to the rights of all the States and Territories and people of the nation, to the inviolability of the Constitution, and the perpetual union, harmony, and prosperity of all—I am most happy to co-operate for the practical success of the principles declared by the convention.[30]

An 1860 campaign banner for Republican presidential candidate Abraham Lincoln and his running mate Hannibal Hamlin. Lincoln's first name is given here as "Abram," a mistake that Republican Party officials seemed unable to correct, much to Lincoln's frustration.

Letter to George Ashmun, *"'ABRAHAM' OR 'ABRAM'"*

Springfield, Ill., June 4, 1860

My dear Sir:—It seems as if the question whether my first name is "Abraham" or "Abram" will never be settled. It is "Abraham," and if the letter of acceptance is not yet in print, you may, if you think fit, have my signature thereto printed "Abraham Lincoln." Exercise your judgment about this.[31]

Letter to Grace Bedell, *"do you not think that people would call it a piece of silly affectation . . . ?"*

Lincoln's response to a letter from a young girl suggesting that he grow a beard.

Springfield, Ill., October 19, 1860

My dear little Miss:—Your very agreeable letter of the 15th is received. I regret the necessity of saying I have no daughter. I have three sons—one seventeen, one nine, and one seven. They with their mother constitute my whole family. As to the whiskers, as I have never worn any, do you not think that people would call it a piece of silly affectation were I to begin wearing them now?[32]

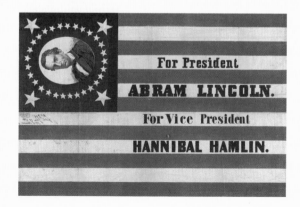

For President
ABRAM LINCOLN.
For Vice President
HANNIBAL HAMLIN.

Letter to Illinois Senator Lyman Trumbull on permitting slavery in the U.S. territories, "Have none of it."

Private, & confidential
Springfield, Ills., Dec. 10, 1860

My dear Sir: Let there be no compromise on the question of extending slavery. If there be, all our labor is lost, and, ere long, must be done again. The dangerous ground—that into which some of our friends have a hankering to run—is Pop. Sov. Have none of it. Stand firm. The tug has to come, & better now, than any time hereafter. Yours as ever[33]

To John A. Gilmer, "May I be pardoned if I ask whether even you have ever attempted to procure the reading of the Republican platform, or my speeches, by the Southern people?"

Gilmer was a member of the U.S. House of Representatives from South Carolina who later became a member of the Confederate Congress.

Strictly confidential.
Dec. 15, 1860

. . . Is it desired that I shall shift the ground upon which I have been elected? I can not do it. You need only to acquaint yourself with that ground, and press it on the attention of

Lyman Trumbull (1813–1896) served in the Illinois House of Representatives in the early 1840s, was appointed a justice of the Supreme Court of Illinois in 1848, and in 1855 was elected a U.S. senator from that state.

An 1860 presidential campaign banner for the Republican ticket, featuring portraits of Abraham Lincoln and vice presidential candidate Hannibal Hamlin, who was a senator from Maine. Oval bust portraits of the two candidates are enclosed in rustic, bent-twig frames, intended perhaps to recall Lincoln's much-publicized backwoods origins. A rail fence appears above the portraits, draped with a banner with the motto, "Free Speech, Free Homes, Free Territory."

the South. It is all in print and easy of access. May I be pardoned if I ask whether even you have ever attempted to procure the reading of the Republican platform, or my speeches, by the Southern people? If not, what reason have I to expect that any additional production of mine would meet a better fate? It would make me appear as if I repented for the crime of having been elected, and was anxious to apologize and beg forgiveness. To so represent me, would be the principal use made of any letter I might now thrust upon the public. My old record cannot be so used; and that is precisely the reason that some new declaration is so much sought.[34]

To Alexander H. Stephens,
"That I suppose is the rub."

For your own eye only.
Springfield, Ills., Dec. 22, 1860
My dear Sir

. . . Do the people of the South really entertain fears that a Republican administration would, directly, or indirectly, interfere with their slaves, or with them, about their slaves? If they do, I wish to assure you, as once a friend, and still, I hope, not an enemy, that there is no cause for such fears.

The South would be in no more danger in this respect, than it was in the days of Washington. I suppose, however, this does not meet the case. You think slavery is right and ought to be extended; while we think it is wrong and ought to be restricted. That I suppose is the rub. It certainly is the only substantial difference between us.[35]

Receipt to Samuel H. Melvin
for the purchase of Lincoln's
home furnishings

February 9, 1861
Bot. of A. Lincoln.

6 Chairs 2 00 12 00
1 Spring Mattress 26 00
1 Wardrobe 20 00
1 Whatnot 10 00
1 Stand 1 50
9 1/2 yds Stair Carpet 50 4 75
4 Comforters 2 00 8 00

———

$82.25
Recd payment
Springfield A. LINCOLN
Feby 9th, 1861[36]

After delivering a heartfelt farewell to hundreds of people who had come to see him off at the Springfield rail depot before his departure for Washington, D.C., Lincoln hastily wrote out a version of the speech for reporters who had missed it. A transcription is on the following page.

Farewell Address at Springfield, Illinois

February 11, 1861

My friends—No one, not in my situation, can appreciate my feeling of sadness at this parting. To this place, and the kindness of these people, I owe every thing. Here I have lived a quarter of a century, and have passed from a young to an old man. Here my children have been born, and one is buried. I now leave, not knowing when, or whether ever, I may return, with a task before me greater than that which rested upon Washington. Without the assistance of that Divine Being, who ever attended him, I cannot succeed. With that assistance I cannot fail. Trusting in Him, who can go with me, and remain with you and be every where for good, let us confidently hope that all will yet be well. To His care commending you, as I hope in your prayers you will commend me, I bid you an affectionate farewell.[37]

Speech from the balcony of the Bates House at Indianapolis, Indiana, "a sort of free-love arrangement . . ."

[February 11, 1861]

. . . But if the Government . . . simply insists upon holding its own forts, or retaking those forts which belong to it,—[cheers,]—or the enforcement of the laws of the United States in the collection of duties upon foreign importations,—[renewed cheers,]—or even the withdrawal of the mails from those portions of the country where the mails themselves are habitually violated; would any or all of these things be coercion? Do the lovers of the Union contend that they will resist coercion or invasion of any State, understanding that any or all of these would be coercing or invading a State? If they do, then it occurs to me that the means for the preservation of the Union they so greatly love, in their own estimation, is of a very thin and airy character. [Applause.] If sick, they would consider the little pills of the homeopathist as already too large for them to swallow. In their view, the Union, as a family relation, would not be anything like a regular marriage at all, but only as a sort of free-love arrangement,—[laughter,]—to be maintained on what that sect calls passionate attraction. [Continued laughter.][38]

Address to the New Jersey
Senate at Trenton, New Jersey

February 21, 1861

. . . I am exceedingly anxious that this Union, the Constitution, and the liberties of the people shall be perpetuated in accordance with the original idea for which that struggle was made, and I shall be most happy indeed if I shall be an humble instrument in the hands of the Almighty, and of this, his almost chosen people, for perpetuating the object of that great struggle. You give me this reception, as I understand, without distinction of party. I learn that this body is composed of a majority of gentlemen who, in the exercise of their best judgment in the choice of a Chief Magistrate, did not think I was the man. I understand, nevertheless, that they came forward here to greet me as the constitutional President of the United States—as citizens of the United States, to meet the man who, for the time being, is the representative man of the nation, united by a purpose to perpetuate the Union and liberties of the people. As such, I accept this reception more gratefully than I could do did I believe it was tendered to me as an individual.[39]

3. "Without Guile, and with Pure Purpose"

The last known full-length portrait of Lincoln prior to his presidency, taken during the summer of 1860.

President-elect Abraham Lincoln raising a flag at Independence Hall, Philadelphia, on February 22, 1861, during his journey to Washington for the inauguration.

After his victory in the presidential election of 1860, Lincoln was greeted with the near-immediate secession of South Carolina from the Union. Within weeks, Mississippi, Florida, Alabama, Georgia, Louisiana, and Texas followed South Carolina's lead. Lincoln's name had not even appeared on the ballot in Southern states.

On March 4, 1861, the new president delivered his first inaugural address (p. 106), a conciliatory speech dedicated to reassuring Southern states that slavery within their borders would not be threatened, appealing to "the mystic chords of memory" and "the better angels of our nature" to maintain the ties of the Union.

To no one's surprise, Lincoln's speech utterly failed to persuade the seceded states to return to the Union. Within weeks, Confederate forces fired on Fort Sumter, in Charleston Harbor, South Carolina, on April 12 after Lincoln, in consultation with his cabinet, sent forces to resupply the federal fort. The first shots of the Civil War had been fired.

William Seward (1801–1872) was the favorite for the Republican presidential nomination in 1860. A popular former governor of New York, later a U.S. senator from that state, and a vocal opponent of slavery, Seward reluctantly but graciously accepted his defeat at the Republican National Convention and campaigned vigorously for Lincoln. When Lincoln appointed him secretary of state, Seward at first chafed under Lincoln's authority, but eventually came to accept and respect him. In 1865, Seward, who had been a target of the group of conspirators led by John Wilkes Booth, was seriously wounded in his home by one of Booth's co-conspirators on the evening of Lincoln's assassination. He recovered from his injuries and continued to serve as secretary of state under Andrew Johnson.

The men whom Lincoln had selected to make up his cabinet—William H. Seward, his secretary of state; Salmon P. Chase at treasury; Simon Cameron, secretary of war; Edward Bates, attorney general among them—had all been contenders for the 1860 Republican presidential nomination, and they tested him as well. It seemed that they sometimes needed reminding that Lincoln, for all his affability, was in charge. His letter to Seward of April 1, 1861, left no doubt about this, and shows the firmness and resolve that would serve Lincoln well both within and outside of his administration. Southern states were treated to the display of Lincoln's determination when he ordered a blockade of their ports and a suspension of habeas corpus in contested areas. Lincoln presented the legal rationale (as well as the strategic necessity) for these actions in his message to a special session of Congress held on July 4, 1861 (p. 118).

A pleasant surprise for Lincoln was that his erstwhile political nemesis, Stephen Douglas, remained steadfast in his loyalty to the Union. Douglas attempted to negotiate with Southern leaders to accept Lincoln's election, and went on a public speaking campaign in support of the Union. But as Douglas died suddenly in June 1861 (see letter to his widow, p. 127). Lincoln had the White House draped in black to honor his lifelong rival.

Ever the cautious lawyer, Lincoln took considerable fire from the abolitionist wing of the Republican party for reversing the emancipation order issued by General John C. Frémont in September 1861. His abiding respect for the rule of law is on display in his letter to Orville H. Browning of September 22, 1861, in which he explains his rationale for reversing the order (p. 124). "If the General needs [slaves]," wrote Lincoln, "he can seize them, and use them; but when the need is past, it is not for him to fix their permanent future condition. That must be settled according to laws made by law-makers, and not by military proclamations."

For many, it is jarring to speak of Lincoln and Karl Marx in the same breath. Yet they were contemporaries, and even had a brief correspondence toward the end of the Civil War. Given his personal biography, it seems quite natural that

Photograph of the inauguration of Abraham Lincoln in front of the east façade of the unfinished U.S. Capitol building, March 4, 1861. Lincoln is standing under the wood canopy, at the front, midway between the left and center posts. His face is in shadow but the white shirtfront is visible.

Lincoln had a clear sympathy for the workingman, though with typical even-handedness, he respected the role of capital and capitalists as well. Still, in his Annual Message to Congress in December 1861 (p. 127), Lincoln shows a surprising familiarity with the ideas of Marx, going so far as to tell Congress that "Labor is prior to, and independent of, capital. . . . Labor is the superior of capital, and deserves much the higher consideration."

Lincoln's principal preoccupation during his presidency very quickly became his role as commander-in-chief of the armed forces. He spent a great deal of time and effort studying military strategy, reading, among other works, General Henry Halleck's *Elements of Military Arts.* In his communications with his generals, Lincoln was nearly always deferential ("Whenever, if at all, in your

judgment, to save yourself and command, a capitulation becomes a necessity, you are authorized to make it"), he wrote to the commander at Fort Sumter on April 4, 1861 (p. 114). As the war progressed and the Union army experienced demoralizing defeats, Lincoln became increasingly confident in offering strategic suggestions and commands, even expressing his frustration to General John C. Frémont for his lack of progress in attacking the railroad near Knoxville (p. 135).

Touchingly, Lincoln always managed to find time for correspondence of a more personal nature. When a famous Union officer who had worked in his law office in Springfield was killed in Virginia, Lincoln wrote a heartfelt personal condolence note to the officer's parents (p. 117). To Lincoln's chagrin, the necessity for this kind of correspondence increased over the course of the war, and the relentless loss of life wore on him as it wore on the nation.

First inaugural address, final text, "the better angels of our nature."

March 4, 1861
Fellow citizens of the United States:

In compliance with a custom as old as the government itself, I appear before you to address you briefly, and to take, in your presence, the oath prescribed by the Constitution of the United States, to be taken by the President "before he enters on the execution of his office."

I do not consider it necessary, at present, for me to discuss those matters of administration about which there is no special anxiety, or excitement.

Apprehension seems to exist among the people of the Southern States, that by the accession of a Republican Administration, their property, and their peace, and personal security, are to be endangered. There has never been any reasonable cause for such apprehension. Indeed, the most ample evidence to the contrary has all the while existed, and been open to their inspection. It is found in nearly all the published speeches of him who now addresses you.

I do but quote from one of those speeches when I declare that "I have no purpose, directly or indirectly, to interfere with the institution of slavery in the States where it exists. I believe I have no lawful right to do so, and I have no inclination to do so." Those who nominated and elected me did so with full knowledge that I had made this, and many similar declarations, and had never recanted them.

. . . I take the official oath to-day, with no mental reservations, and with no purpose to construe the Constitution or laws, by any hypercritical rules. And while I do not choose now to specify particular acts of Congress as proper to be enforced, I do suggest, that it will be much safer for all, both in official and private stations, to conform to, and abide by, all those acts which stand unrepealed, than to violate any of them, trusting to find impunity in having them held to be unconstitutional.

It is seventy-two years since the first inauguration of a President under our national Constitution. During that period fifteen different and greatly distinguished citizens, have, in succession, administered the executive branch of the government. They have conducted it through many perils; and, generally, with great success. Yet, with all this scope for precedent, I now enter upon the same task for the brief constitutional term of four years, under great and peculiar difficulty. A disruption of the Federal Union heretofore only menaced, is now formidably attempted.

I hold, that in contemplation of universal law, and of the Constitution, the Union of these States is perpetual. Perpetuity is implied, if not expressed, in the fundamental law of all national governments. It is safe to assert that no government proper, ever had a provision in its organic law for its own termination. Continue to execute all the express provisions of our national Constitution, and the Union will endure forever—it being impossible to destroy it, except by some action not provided for in the instrument itself.

Again, if the United States be not a government proper, but an association of States in the nature of contract merely, can it, as a contract, be peaceably unmade, by less than all the parties who made it? One party to a contract may violate it—break it, so to speak; but does it not require all to lawfully rescind it?

. . . In doing this there needs to be no bloodshed or violence; and there shall be none, unless it be forced upon the national authority. The power confided to me, will be used to hold, occupy, and possess the property, and places belonging to the government, and to collect the duties and imposts; but beyond what may be necessary for these objects, there will be no invasion—no using of force against, or among the people anywhere. Where hostility to the United States, in any interior locality, shall be so great and so universal, as to prevent competent resident citizens from holding the Federal offices, there will be no attempt to force obnoxious strangers among the people for that object. While the strict legal right may exist in the government to enforce the exercise of these offices, the attempt to do so would be so irritating, and so nearly impracticable with all, that I deem it better to forego, for the time, the uses of such offices.

The mails, unless repelled, will continue to be furnished in all parts of the Union. So far as possible, the people everywhere shall have that sense of perfect security which is most favorable to calm thought and reflection. The course here indicated will be followed, unless current events, and experience, shall show a modification, or change, to be proper; and in every case and exigency, my best discretion will be exercised, according to circumstances actually existing, and with a view and a hope of a peaceful solution of the national troubles, and the restoration of fraternal sympathies and affections.

... All profess to be content in the Union, if all constitutional rights can be maintained. Is it true, then, that any right, plainly written in the Constitution, has been denied? I think not. Happily the human mind is so constituted, that no party can reach to the audacity of doing this. Think, if you can, of a single instance in which a plainly written provision of the Constitution has ever been denied. If, by the mere force of numbers, a majority should deprive a minority of any clearly written constitutional right, it might, in a moral point of view, justify revolution—certainly would, if such right were a vital one. But such is not our case. All the vital rights of minorities, and of individuals, are so plainly assured to them, by affirmations and negations, guarranties and prohibitions, in the Constitution, that controversies never arise concerning them. But no organic law can ever be framed with a provision specifically applicable to every question which may occur in practical administration. No foresight can anticipate, nor any document of reasonable length contain express provisions for all possible questions. Shall fugitives from labor be surrendered by national or by State authority? The Constitution does not expressly say. May Congress prohibit slavery in the territories? The Constitution does not expressly say. Must Congress protect slavery in the territories? The Constitution does not expressly say.

From questions of this class spring all our constitutional controversies, and we divide upon them into majorities and minorities. If the minority will not acquiesce, the majority must, or the government must cease. There is no other alternative; for continuing the government, is acquiescence on one side or the other. If a minority, in such case, will secede rather than acquiesce, they make a precedent which, in turn, will divide and ruin them; for a minority of their own will secede from them, whenever a majority refuses to be controlled by such minority. For instance, why may not any portion of a new confederacy, a year or two hence, arbitrarily secede again, precisely as portions of the present Union now claim to secede from it. All who cherish disunion sentiments, are now being educated to the exact temper of doing this. Is there such perfect identity of interests among the States to compose a new Union, as to produce harmony only, and prevent renewed secession?

Plainly, the central idea of secession, is the essence of anarchy. A majority, held in restraint by constitutional checks, and limitations, and always changing easily, with deliberate changes of popular opinions and sentiments, is the only true sovereign of a free people. Whoever rejects it, does, of necessity, fly to anarchy or to despotism. Unanimity is impossible; the rule of a minority, as a permanent arrangement, is wholly inadmissable; so that, rejecting the majority principle, anarchy, or despotism in some form, is all that is left.

. . . One section of our country believes slavery is right, and ought to be extended, while the other believes it is wrong, and ought not to be extended. This is the only substantial dispute.

. . . Physically speaking, we cannot separate. We cannot remove our respective sections from each other, nor build an impassable wall between them. A husband and wife may be divorced, and go out of the presence, and beyond the reach of each other; but the different parts of our country cannot do this. They cannot but remain face to face; and intercourse, either amicable or hostile, must continue between them. Is it possible then to make that intercourse more advantageous, or more satisfactory, after separation than before? Can aliens make treaties easier than friends can make laws? Can treaties be more faithfully enforced between aliens, than laws can among friends? Suppose you go to war, you cannot fight always; and when, after much loss on both sides, and no gain on either, you cease fighting, the identical old questions, as to terms of intercourse, are again upon you.

This country, with its institutions, belongs to the people who inhabit it. Whenever they shall grow weary of the existing government, they can exercise their constitutional right of amending it, or their revolutionary right to dismember, or overthrow it. I can not be ignorant of the fact that many worthy, and patriotic citizens are desirous of having the national constitution amended. While I make no recommendation of amendments, I fully recognize the rightful authority of the people over the whole subject, to be exercised in either of the modes prescribed in the instrument itself; and I should, under existing circumstances, favor, rather than oppose, a fair oppertunity [sic] being afforded the people to act upon it.

. . . Why should there not be a patient confidence in the ultimate justice of the people? Is there any better, or equal hope, in the world? In our present differences, is either party without faith of being in the right? If the Almighty

Ruler of nations, with his eternal truth and justice, be on your side of the North, or on yours of the South, that truth, and that justice, will surely prevail, by the judgment of this great tribunal, the American people.

. . . My countrymen, one and all, think calmly and well, upon this whole subject. Nothing valuable can be lost by taking time. If there be an object to hurry any of you, in hot haste, to a step which you would never take deliberately, that

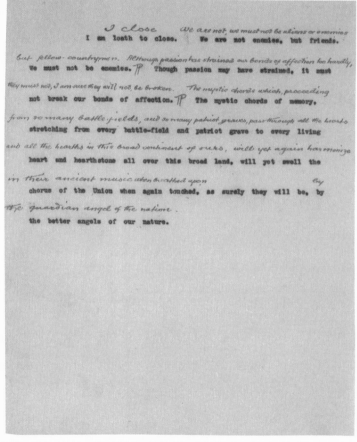

William Seward suggested to Lincoln that he close the inaugural address on a conciliatory note. His handwritten words are shown here, juxtaposed with the words that Lincoln ultimately chose.

improved, I make no recommendations of amendments. I am, rather, for the old ship, and the chart of the old pilots. If, however, the people desire a new, or an altered vessel, the matter is exclusively their own, and they can move in the premises, as well without as with an executive recommendation. I shall place no obstacle in the way of what may appear to be their wishes.

The Chief Magistrate derives all his authority from the people, and they have conferred none upon him to fix terms for the separation of the States. The people themselves can do this *also* if they choose; but the executive, as such, has nothing to do with it. His duty is to administer the present government, as it came to his hands, and to transmit it, unimpaired by him, to his successor.

Why should there not be a patient confidence in the ultimate justice of the people? Is there any better or equal hope, in the world? In our present differences, is either party without faith *of being* in the right? If the Almighty Ruler of nations, with his eternal truth and justice, be on *on your side of the North, or on yours of the South,* that truth and that justice will surely prevail, by the judgment of this great tribunal, the American people.

By the frame of the government under which we live, this same people have wisely given their public servants but little power for mischief; and have, with equal wisdom, provided for the return of that little to their own hands at very short intervals. *retain their virtue, and vigilence, no administration* While the people by any extreme of wickedness or folly, can very seriously injure the government, in the short space of four years.

My countrymen, one and all, *think calmly and* well, upon this whole subject. Nothing valuable can be lost by taking time. If there be an object to *hurry* any of you, in hot haste, to a step which you would never take *deliberately*, that object will be frustrated by taking time; but no good object can be frustrated by it. Such of you as are now dissatisfied, still have the old Constitution unimpaired, and, on the sensitive point, the laws of your own framing under it; while the new administration will have no immediate power, if it would, to change either. If it were admitted that you who are dissatisfied, hold the right side in the dispute, there still is no single good reason for precipitate action. Intelligence, patriotism, Christianity, and a firm reliance on Him, who has never yet forsaken this favored land, are still competent to adjust, in the best way, all our present difficulty.

In your hands, my dissatisfied fellow countrymen, and not in *mine*, is the momentous issue of civil war. The government will not assail *you*. You can have no conflict, without being yourselves the aggressors. You have no oath registered in Heaven to destroy the government, while *I* shall have the most solemn one to "preserve, protect and defend" it.

I am loth to close. We are not enemies, but friends— We must not be enemies. Though passion may have strained, it must not break our bonds of affection. The mystic chords of memory, stretching from every battle-field, and patriot grave, to every living heart and hearth-stone, all over this broad land, will yet swell the chorus of the Union, when again touched, as surely they will be, by the better angels of our nature.

The final draft of Lincoln's first inaugural speech shows his handwritten emendations to the text, including the famous final paragraph invoking "the better angels of our nature."

object will be frustrated by taking time; but no good object can be frustrated by it. Such of you as are now dissatisfied, still have the old Constitution unimpaired, and, on the sensitive point, the laws of your own framing under it; while the new administration will have no immediate power, if it would, to change either. If it were admitted that you who are dissatisfied, hold the right side in the dispute, there still is no single good reason for precipitate action. Intelligence, patriotism, Christianity, and a firm reliance on Him, who has never yet forsaken this favored land, are still competent to adjust, in the best way, all our present difficulty.

In your hands, my dissatisfied fellow countrymen, and not in mine, is the momentous issue of civil war. The government will not assail you. You can have no conflict, without being yourselves the aggressors. You have no oath registered in Heaven to destroy the government, while I shall have the most solemn one to "preserve, protect and defend" it.

I am loth to close. We are not enemies, but friends. We must not be enemies. Though passion may have strained, it must not break our bonds of affection. The mystic chords of memory, streching from every battle-field, and patriot grave, to every living heart and hearthstone, all over this broad land, will yet swell the chorus of the Union, when again touched, as surely they will be, by the better angels of our nature.[1]

Letter to William H. Seward, "When a general line of policy is adopted, I apprehend there is no danger of its being changed without good reason . . ."

Seward, Lincoln's one-time political rival, was now secretary of state in Lincoln's cabinet.

Executive Mansion, April 1, 1861

My dear Sir: Since parting with you I have been considering your paper dated this day, and entitled "Some thoughts for the President's consideration." The first proposition in it is, "1st. We are at the end of a month's administration, and yet without a policy, either domestic or foreign."

At the beginning of that month, in the inaugeral, I said "The power confided to me will be used to hold, occupy and possess the property and places belonging to the government, and to collect the duties, and imposts." This had your distinct approval at the time; and, taken in connection with the order I immediately gave General Scott, directing him to employ every means in his power to strengthen and hold the forts, comprises the exact domestic policy you now urge . . .

When a general line of policy is adopted, I apprehend there is no danger of its being changed without good reason, or continuing to be a subject of unnecessary debate; still, upon points arising in its progress, I wish, and suppose I am entitled to have the advice of all the cabinet.[2]

Lincoln's reply to a memorandum from Secretary of State William H. Seward shows the president's uncanny ability to simultaneously be assertive and humble. Seward had implied that Lincoln had yet to form a domestic or foreign policy, an assertion to which Lincoln took polite but firm exception.

Orders to Robert Anderson, "Whenever, if at all, in your judgment, to save yourself and command, a capitulation becomes a necessity, you are authorized to make it."

Anderson was the commander of federal troops in South Carolina and, as such, was responsible for the defense of Fort Sumter. He was a proslavery Kentuckian who had remained loyal to the Union.

[War Department] Washington, April 4, 1861

Sir: Your letter of the 1st. inst. occasions some anxiety to the President.

On the information of Capt. Fox, he had supposed you could hold out till the 15th. inst. without any great inconvenience; and had prepared an expedition to relieve you before that period.

Hoping still that you will be able to sustain yourself till the 11th. or 12th. inst. the expedition will go forward; and, finding your flag flying, will attempt to provision you, and, in case the effort is resisted, will endeavor also to reinforce you.

You will therefore hold out if possible till the arrival of the expedition.

It is not, however, the intention of the President to subject your command to any danger or hardship beyond what, in your judgement, would be usual in military life; and he has entire confidence that you will act as becomes a patriot and a soldier, under all circumstances.

Whenever, if at all, in your judgment, to save yourself and command, a capitulation becomes a necessity, you are authorized to make it. [Respectfully SIMON CAMERON.]

[To Major Robert Anderson U. S. Army]

This was sent by Capt. Talbot, on April 6, 1861, to be delivered to Maj. Anderson, if permitted. On reaching Charleston, he was refused permission to deliver it to Major Anderson.[3]

Proclamation calling militia and convening Congress, "I appeal to all loyal citizens . . ."

April 15, 1861
By the President of the United States
A Proclamation.

Whereas the laws of the United States have been for some time past, and now are opposed, and the execution thereof obstructed, in the States of South Carolina, Georgia, Alabama, Florida, Mississippi, Louisiana and Texas, by combinations too powerful to be suppressed by the ordinary course of judicial proceedings, or by the powers vested in the Marshals by law,

Now therefore, I, Abraham Lincoln, President of the United States, in virtue of the power in me vested by the Constitution, and the laws, have thought fit to call forth, and hereby do call forth, the militia of the several States of the Union, to the aggregate number of seventy-five thousand, in order to suppress said combinations, and to cause the laws to be duly executed. The details, for this object, will be immediately communicated to the State authorities through the War Department.

I appeal to all loyal citizens to favor, facilitate and aid this effort to maintain the honor, the integrity, and the existence of our National Union, and the perpetuity of popular government; and to redress wrongs already long enough endured.

I deem it proper to say that the first service assigned to the forces hereby called forth will probably be to re-possess the forts, places, and property which have been seized from the Union; and in every event, the utmost care will be observed, consistently with the objects aforesaid, to avoid any devastation, any destruction of, or interference with, property, or any disturbance of peaceful citizens in any part of the country.

And I hereby command the persons composing the combinations aforesaid to disperse, and retire peaceably to their respective abodes within twenty days from this date . . .[4]

3

Washington D.C.
May 25. 1861

To the Father and Mother of Col. Elmer E.
Ellsworth:

My Dear Sir and Madam.

In the untimely loss
of your noble son, our affliction here is scarcely
less than your own. So much of promised
usefulness to one's country, and of bright
hopes for one's self and friends, have rarely
been so suddenly dashed as in his fall.
In size, in years, and in youthful appearance a boy only, his power to command
men was surpassingly great. This
power combined with a fine intellect,
an indomitable energy, and a taste
altogether military, constituted in him,
as seemed to me the best natural talent,
in that department, I ever knew.

And yet he was singularly modest
and deferential in social intercourse. My
acquaintance with him began less than two years
ago; yet through the latter half of the

To Ephraim D. and Phoebe Ellsworth, "In the hope that it may be no intrusion upon the sacredness of your sorrow . . ."

Ephraim and Phoebe Ellsworth were the parents of Elmer Ellsworth, the first Union officer killed in the Civil War. A former clerk in Lincoln's Springfield law office who had grown close to Lincoln, Ellsworth was killed while removing a Confederate flag from a building in Alexandria, Virginia, at Lincoln's behest.

Washington, D.C. , May 25, 1861
To the Father and Mother of Col. Elmer E. Ellsworth:

My dear Sir and Madam, In the untimely loss of your noble son, our affliction here, is scarcely less than your own. So much of promised usefulness to one's country, and of bright hopes for one's self and friends, have rarely been so suddenly dashed, as in his fall. In size, in years, and in youthful appearance, a boy only, his power to command men, was surpassingly great. This power, combined with a fine intellect, an indomitable energy, and a taste altogether military, constituted in him, as seemed to me, the best natural talent, in that department, I ever knew. And yet he was singularly modest and deferential in social intercourse. My acquaintance with him began less than two years ago; yet through the latter half of the intervening period, it was as intimate as the disparity of our ages, and my engrossing engagements, would permit. To me, he appeared to have no indulgences or pastimes; and I never heard him utter a profane, or an intemperate word. What was conclusive of his good heart, he never forgot his parents. The honors he labored for so laudably, and, in the sad end, so gallantly gave his life, he meant for them, no less than for himself.

In the hope that it may be no intrusion upon the sacredness of your sorrow, I have ventured to address you this tribute to the memory of my young friend, and your brave and early fallen child.

May God give you that consolation which is beyond all earthly power. Sincerely your friend in a common affliction[.][5]

The White House copy of Lincoln's condolence letter, sent to the parents of Elmer Ellsworth in May 1861.

Message to Congress in
special session, "without guile,
and with pure purpose . . ."

July 4, 1861
Fellow-citizens of the Senate and House of Representatives:

. . . At the beginning of the present Presidential term, four months ago, the functions of the Federal Government were found to be generally suspended within the several States of South Carolina, Georgia, Alabama, Mississippi, Louisiana, and Florida, excepting only those of the Post Office Department.

Within these States, all the Forts, Arsenals, Dock-yards, Customhouses, and the like, including the movable and stationary property in, and about them, had been seized, and were held in open hostility to this Government, excepting only Forts Pickens, Taylor, and Jefferson, on, and near the Florida coast, and Fort Sumter, in Charleston harbor, South Carolina. The Forts thus seized had been put in improved condition; new ones had been built; and armed forces had been organized, and were organizing, all avowedly with the same hostile purpose.

. . . the assault upon, and reduction of, Fort Sumter, was, in no sense, a matter of self defence on the part of the assailants. They well knew that the garrison in the Fort could, by no possibility, commit aggression upon them. They knew—they were expressly notified—that the giving of bread to the few brave and hungry men of the garrison, was all which would on that occasion be attempted, unless themselves, by resisting so much, should provoke more. They knew that this Government desired to keep the garrison in the Fort, not to assail them, but merely to maintain visible possession, and thus to preserve the Union from actual, and immediate dissolution—trusting, as herein-before stated, to time, discussion, and the ballot-box, for final adjustment; and they assailed, and reduced the Fort, for precisely the reverse object—to drive out the visible authority of the Federal Union, and thus force it to immediate dissolution.

That this was their object, the Executive well understood; and having said to them in the inaugural address, "You can have no conflict without being yourselves the aggressors," he took pains, not only to keep this declaration good, but also to keep the case so free from the power of ingenious sophistry, as that the world should not be able to misunderstand it. By the affair at

Fort Sumter, with its surrounding circumstances, that point was reached. Then, and thereby, the assailants of the Government, began the conflict of arms, without a gun in sight, or in expectancy, to return their fire, save only the few in the Fort, sent to that harbor, years before, for their own protection, and still ready to give that protection, in whatever was lawful. In this act, discarding all else, they have forced upon the country, the distinct issue: "Immediate dissolution, or blood."

And this issue embraces more than the fate of these United States. It presents to the whole family of man, the question, whether a constitutional republic, or a democracy—a government of the people, by the same people—can, or cannot, maintain its territorial integrity, against its own domestic foes. It presents the question, whether discontented individuals, too few in numbers to control administration, according to organic law, in any case, can always, upon the pretences made in this case, or on any other pretences, or arbitrarily, without any pretence, break up their Government, and thus practically put an end to free government upon the earth. It forces us to ask: "Is there, in all republics, this inherent, and fatal weakness?" "Must a government, of necessity, be too strong for the liberties of its own people, or too weak to maintain its own existence?"

So viewing the issue, no choice was left but to call out the war power of the Government; and so to resist force, employed for its destruction, by force, for its preservation.

. . . Soon after the first call for militia, it was considered a duty to authorize the Commanding General, in proper cases, according to his discretion, to suspend the privilege of the writ of habeas corpus; or, in other words, to arrest, and detain, without resort to the ordinary processes and forms of law, such individuals as he might deem dangerous to the public safety. This authority has purposely been exercised but very sparingly. . . . The provision of the Constitution that "The privilege of the writ of habeas corpus, shall not be suspended unless when, in cases of rebellion or invasion, the public safety may require it," is equivalent to a provision—is a provision—that such privilege may be suspended when, in cases of rebellion, or invasion, the public safety does require it. It was decided that we have a case of rebellion, and that the public safety does require the qualified suspension of the privilege of the writ which was authorized to be made.

. . . It might seem, at first thought, to be of little difference whether the present movement at the South be called "secession" or "rebellion." The movers, however, well understand the difference. At the beginning, they knew they could never raise their treason to any respectable magnitude, by any name which implies violation of law. . . . They invented an ingenious sophism, which, if conceded, was followed by perfectly logical steps, through all the incidents, to the complete destruction of the Union.

. . . This sophism derives much—perhaps the whole—of its currency, from the assumption, that there is some omnipotent, and sacred supremacy, pertaining to a State—to each State of our Federal Union. Our States have neither more, nor less power, than that reserved to them, in the Union, by the Constitution—no one of them ever having been a State out of the Union. The original ones passed into the Union even before they cast off their British colonial dependence; and the new ones each came into the Union directly from a condition of dependence, excepting Texas. And even Texas, in its temporary independence, was never designated a State. The new ones only took the designation of States, on coming into the Union, while that name was first adopted for the old ones, in, and by, the Declaration of Independence. . . . Having never been States, either in substance, or in name, outside of the Union, whence this magical omnipotence of "State rights," asserting a claim of power to lawfully destroy the Union itself? Much is said about the "sovereignty" of the States; but the word, even, is not in the national Constitution; nor, as is believed, in any of the State constitutions. What is a "sovereignty," in the political sense of the term? Would it be far wrong to define it "A political community, without a political superior"? Tested by this, no one of our States, except Texas, ever was a sovereignty. And even Texas gave up the character on coming into the Union; by which act, she acknowledged the Constitution of the United States, and the laws and treaties of the

Retouched photograph of Lincoln reading to his son Tad (1853–1871). Tad, who was deeply adored by Lincoln, was an unruly but welcome presence in the White House. He died at age eighteen, possibly of tuberculosis.

United States made in pursuance of the Constitution, to be, for her, the supreme law of the land. The States have their status IN the Union, and they have no other legal status. If they break from this, they can only do so against law, and by revolution.

. . . Unquestionably the States have the powers, and rights, reserved to them in, and by the National Constitution; but among these, surely, are not included all conceivable powers, however mischievous, or destructive; but, at most, such only, as were known in the world, at the time, as governmental powers; and certainly, a power to destroy the government itself, had never been known as a governmental—as a merely administrative power. This relative matter of National power, and State rights, as a principle, is no other than the principle of generality, and locality. Whatever concerns the whole, should be confided to the whole—to the general government; while, whatever concerns only the State, should be left exclusively, to the State. This is all there is of original principle about it. Whether the National Constitution, in defining boundaries between the two, has applied the principle with exact accuracy, is not to be questioned. We are all bound by that defining, without question.

. . . The seceders insist that our Constitution admits of secession. They have assumed to make a National Constitution of their own, in which, of necessity, they have either discarded, or retained, the right of secession, as they insist, it exists in ours. If they have discarded it, they thereby admit that, on principle, it ought not to be in ours. If they have retained it, by their own construction of ours they show that to be consistent they must secede from one another, whenever they shall find it the easiest way of settling their debts, or effecting any other selfish, or unjust object. The principle itself is one of disintegration, and upon which no government can possibly endure.

. . . This is essentially a People's contest. On the side of the Union, it is a struggle for maintaining in the world, that form, and substance of government, whose leading object is, to elevate the condition of men—to lift artificial weights from all shoulders—to clear the paths of laudable pursuit for all—to afford all, an unfettered start, and a fair chance, in the race of life. Yielding to partial, and temporary departures, from necessity, this is the leading object of the government for whose existence we contend.

. . . Our popular government has often been called an experiment. Two points in it, our people have already settled—the successful establishing, and the successful administering of it. One still remains—its successful maintenance against a formidable [internal] attempt to overthrow it. It is now for them to demonstrate to the world, that those who can fairly carry an election, can also suppress a rebellion—that ballots are the rightful, and peaceful, successors of bullets; and that when ballots have fairly, and constitutionally, decided, there can be no successful appeal, back to bullets; that there can be no successful appeal, except to ballots themselves, at succeeding elections. Such will be a great lesson of peace; teaching men that what they cannot take by an election, neither can they take it by a war—teaching all, the folly of being the beginners of a war.

. . . And having thus chosen our course, without guile, and with pure purpose, let us renew our trust in God, and go forward without fear, and with manly hearts.[6]

Proclamation of a National Fast Day

August 12, 1861
By the President of the United States of America:
A Proclamation.

. . . whereas, when our own beloved Country, once, by the blessing of God, united, prosperous and happy, is now afflicted with faction and civil war, it is peculiarly fit for us to recognize the hand of God in this terrible visitation, and in sorrowful remembrance of our own faults and crimes as a nation and as individuals, to humble ourselves before Him, and to pray for His mercy,—to pray that we may be spared further punishment, though most justly deserved; that our arms may be blessed and made effectual for the re-establishment of law, order and peace, throughout the wide extent of our country; and that the inestimable boon of civil and religious liberty, earned under His guidance and blessing, by the labors and sufferings of our fathers, may be restored in all its original excellence:—

Therefore, I, Abraham Lincoln, President of the United States, do appoint the last Thursday in September next, as a day of humiliation, prayer and fasting for all the people of the nation. And I do earnestly recommend to all the People, and especially to all ministers and teachers of religion of all denominations, and to all heads of families, to observe and keep that day according to their several creeds and modes of worship, in all humility and with all religious solemnity, to the end that the united prayer of the nation may ascend to the Throne of Grace and bring down plentiful blessings upon our Country.[7]

Confidential letter to Major General John C. Frémont, "This letter is written in a spirit of caution and not of censure."

Frémont, the Union commander of the Western Armies, had issued a proclamation freeing the slaves in his district without authorization from the president or Congress.

Private and confidential.
Washington, D.C., Sept. 2, 1861

My dear Sir: Two points in your proclamation of August 30th give me some anxiety. First, should you shoot a man, according to the proclamation, the Confederates would very certainly shoot our best man in their hands in retaliation; and so, man for man, indefinitely. It is therefore my order that you allow no man to be shot, under the proclamation, without first having my approbation or consent.

Portrait of Major General John C. Frémont (1813–1890). Popularly known as "The Pathfinder" because of his numerous expeditions in the American West during the 1840s (note that the border art at top left includes Pike's Peak), Frémont, an opponent of slavery, was also known as something of a loose cannon. During the Mexican-Amercian War, as a major in the U.S. Army, Frémont briefly declared himself military governor of California, a self-bestowed privilege for which he was court-martialed and convicted. Pardoned by President James A. Polk, Frémont reentered public life, eventually becoming the Republican presidential candidate in 1856. Lincoln had campaigned for him. Lincoln appointed him commander of the Western Armies in July 1861.

Secondly, I think there is great danger that the closing paragraph, in relation to the confiscation of property, and the liberating slaves of traiterous owners, will alarm our Southern Union friends, and turn them against us— perhaps ruin our rather fair prospect for Kentucky. Allow me therefore to ask, that you will as of your own motion, modify that paragraph so as to conform to the first and fourth sections of the act of Congress, entitled, "An act to confiscate property used for insurrectionary purposes," approved August, 6th, 1861, and a copy of which act I herewith send you. This letter is written in a spirit of caution and not of censure.

I send it by a special messenger, in order that it may certainly and speedily reach you.[8]

To Orville H. Browning, "The proclamation in the point in question, is simply 'dictatorship.'"

Lincoln explains his rationale for overturning a military order, issued by General John C. Frémont, freeing the slaves in Missouri.

Private & confidential.
Executive Mansion, Washington, Sept 22d, 1861.
My dear Sir

Yours of the 17th is just received; and coming from you, I confess it astonishes me. That you should object to my adhering to a law, which you had assisted in making, and presenting to me, less than a month before, is odd enough. But this is a very small part. Genl. Frémont's proclamation, as to confiscation of property, and the liberation of slaves, is purely political, and not within the range of military law, or necessity. If a commanding General finds a necessity to seize the farm of a private owner, for a pasture, an encampment, or a fortification, he has the right to do so, and to so hold it, as long as the necessity lasts; and this is within military law, because within military necessity. But to say the farm shall no longer belong to the owner, or his heirs forever; and this as well when the farm is not needed for military purposes as when it is, is purely political, without the savor of military law about it. And the same is true of slaves. If the General needs them, he can seize them, and use them; but when the need is past, it is not for him to fix their permanent future condition. That must be settled according to laws made by law-makers, and not by military proclamations. The proclamation in the point in question, is simply "dictatorship." It assumes that the general may do anything he pleases—confiscate the lands and free the slaves of loyal people, as well as of disloyal ones. And going the whole figure I have no doubt would be more popular with some thoughtless people, than that which has been done! But I cannot assume this reckless position; nor allow others to assume it on my responsibility. You speak of it as being the only means of saving the government. On the contrary it is itself the surrender of the government. Can it be pretended that it is any longer the government of the U.S.—any government of Constitution and laws,—wherein a General, or a President, may make permanent rules of property by proclamation?

I do not say Congress might not with propriety pass a law, on the point, just such as General Frémont proclaimed. I do not say I might not, as a member of Congress, vote for it. What I object to, is, that I as President, shall expressly or impliedly seize and exercise the permanent legislative functions of the government.

So much as to principle. Now as to policy. No doubt the thing was popular in some quarters, and would have been more so if it had been a general declaration of emancipation. The Kentucky Legislature would not budge till that proclamation was modified; and Gen. Anderson telegraphed me that on the news of Gen. Frémont having actually issued deeds of manumission, a whole company of our Volunteers threw down their arms and disbanded. I was so assured, as to think it probable, that the very arms we had furnished Kentucky would be turned against us. I think to lose Kentucky is nearly the same as to lose the whole game. Kentucky gone, we can not hold Missouri, nor, as I think, Maryland. These all against us, and the job on our hands is too large for us. We would as well consent to separation at once, including the surrender of this capitol. On the contrary, if you will give up your restlessness for new positions, and back me manfully on the grounds upon which you and other kind friends gave me the election, and have approved in my public documents, we shall go through triumphantly.

You must not understand I took my course on the proclamation because of Kentucky. I took the same ground in a private letter to General Frémont before I heard from Kentucky.

You think I am inconsistent because I did not also forbid Gen. Frémont to shoot men under the proclamation. I understand that part to be within military law; but I also think, and so privately wrote Gen. Frémont, that it is impolitic in this, that our adversaries have the power, and will certainly exercise it, to shoot as many of our men as we shoot of theirs. I did not say this in the public letter, because it is a subject I prefer not to discuss in the hearing of our enemies.

There has been no thought of removing Gen. Frémont on any ground connected with his proclamation; and if there has been any wish for his removal on any ground, our mutual friend Sam. Glover [a St. Louis attorney and a friend of Lincoln's] can probably tell you what it was. I hope no real necessity for it exists on any ground.[9]

Inscription on a photograph given to Mrs. Lucy G. Speed

Lucy Speed was the mother of Lincoln's closest friend, Joshua Speed.

For Mrs. Lucy G. Speed, from whose pious hand I accepted the present of an Oxford Bible twenty years ago.
    Washington, D.C., October 3, 1861[10]

Lincoln inscribed this photograph to the mother of his friend Joshua Speed on October 3, 1861. Mrs. Speed had consoled Lincoln during the depression he had experienced following his breakup with Mary Todd in January 1841, when she had given him the copy of the Bible he alludes to in his inscription.

Advice to Mrs. Stephen A. Douglas, "it is especially dangerous for my name to be connected with the matter . . ."

Adele Cutts Douglas was the widow of Stephen A. Douglas. She was the guardian of Douglas's young children from his first marriage to a Southern woman, which had ended with his first wife's death. Stephen Douglas had died of typhoid fever in June 1861.

Executive Mansion, Nov. 27, 1861

Yesterday Mrs. Douglas called, saying she is guardian of the minor children of her late husband; that she is being urged, against her inclination, to send them South, on the plea of avoiding the confiscation of their property there, and asking my counsel in the case.

I expect the United States will overcome the attempt to confiscate property, because of loyalty to the government; but if not, I still do not expect the property of absent minor children will be confiscated. I therefore think Mrs. Douglas may safely act her pleasure in the premises.

But it is especially dangerous for my name to be connected with the matter; for nothing would more certainly excite the secessionists to do the worst they can against the children.[11]

Annual Message to Congress, "let us proceed in the great task which events have devolved upon us."

December 3, 1861
Fellow Citizens of the Senate and House of Representatives:

In the midst of unprecedented political troubles, we have cause of great gratitude to God for unusual good health, and most abundant harvests.

You will not be surprised to learn that, in the peculiar exigencies of the times, our intercourse with foreign nations has been attended with profound solicitude, chiefly turning upon our own domestic affairs.

A disloyal portion of the American people have, during the whole year, been engaged in an attempt to divide and destroy the Union.

... The last ray of hope for preserving the Union peaceably, expired at the assault upon Fort Sumter; and a general review of what has occurred since may not be unprofitable. What was painfully uncertain then, is much better defined and more distinct now; and the progress of events is plainly in the right direction. The insurgents confidently claimed a strong support from north of Mason and Dixon's line; and the friends of the Union were not free from apprehension on the point. This, however, was soon settled definitely and on the right side. South of the line, noble little Delaware led off right from the first. Maryland was made to seem against the Union. Our soldiers were assaulted, bridges were burned, and railroads torn up, within her limits; and we were many days, at one time, without the ability to bring a single regiment over her soil to the capital. Now, her bridges and railroads are repaired and open to the government; she already gives seven regiments to the cause of the Union and none to the enemy; and her people, at a regular election, have sustained the Union, by a larger majority, and a larger aggregate vote than they ever before gave to any candidate, or any question. Kentucky, too, for some time in doubt, is now decidedly, and, I think, unchangeably, ranged on the side of the Union. Missouri is comparatively quiet; and I believe cannot again be overrun by the insurrectionists. These three States of Maryland, Kentucky, and Missouri, neither of which would promise a single soldier at first, have now an aggregate of not less than forty thousand in the field, for the Union; while, of their citizens, certainly not more than a third of that number, and they of doubtful whereabouts, and doubtful existence, are in arms against it. After a somewhat bloody struggle of months, winter closes on the Union people of western Virginia, leaving them masters of their own country.

... It is not needed, nor fitting here, that a general argument should be made in favor of popular institutions; but there is one point, with its connexions, not so hackneyed as most others, to which I ask a brief attention. It is the effort to place capital on an equal footing with, if not above labor, in the structure of government. It is assumed that labor is available only in connexion with capital; that nobody labors unless somebody else, owning capital, somehow by the use of it, induces him to labor. This assumed, it is next considered whether it is best that capital shall hire laborers, and thus induce them to work by their own consent, or buy them, and drive them to it without their consent. Having proceeded so far, it is naturally concluded that all laborers are either hired laborers, or what we call slaves. And further it is assumed that whoever is once a hired laborer, is fixed in that condition for life.

Now, there is no such relation between capital and labor as assumed; nor is there any such thing as a free man being fixed for life in the condition of a hired laborer. Both these assumptions are false, and all inferences from them are groundless.

Labor is prior to, and independent of, capital. Capital is only the fruit of labor, and could never have existed if labor had not first existed. Labor is the superior of capital, and deserves much the higher consideration. Capital has its rights, which are as worthy of protection as any other rights.

. . . Again: as has already been said, there is not, of necessity, any such thing as the free hired laborer being fixed to that condition for life. Many independent men everywhere in these States, a few years back in their lives, were hired laborers. The prudent, penniless beginner in the world, labors for wages awhile, saves a surplus with which to buy tools or land for himself; then labors on his own account another while, and at length hires another new beginner to help him. This is the just, and generous, and prosperous system, which opens the way to all—gives hope to all, and consequent energy, and progress, and improvement of condition to all. No men living are more worthy to be trusted than those who toil up from poverty—none less inclined to take, or touch, aught which they have not honestly earned. Let them beware of surrendering a political power which they already possess, and which, if surrendered, will surely be used to close the door of advancement against such as they, and to fix new disabilities and burdens upon them, till all of liberty shall be lost.

From the first taking of our national census to the last are seventy years; and we find our population at the end of the period eight times as great as it was at the beginning. The increase of those other things which men deem desirable has been even greater. We thus have at one view, what the popular principle applied to government, through the machinery of the States and the Union, has produced in a given time; and also what, if firmly maintained, it promises for the future. There are already among us those, who, if the Union be preserved, will live to see it contain two hundred and fifty millions. The struggle of today, is not altogether for today—it is for a vast future also. With a reliance on Providence, all the more firm and earnest, let us proceed in the great task which events have devolved upon us.[12]

To Mrs. Susannah Weathers, "A pair of socks so fine, and soft, and warm . . ."

Executive Mansion, Washington, Dec. 4, 1861.
My dear Madam

I take great pleasure in acknowledging the receipt of your letter of Nov. 26; and in thanking you for the present by which it was accompanied. A pair of socks so fine, and soft, and warm, could hardly have been manufactured in any other way than the old Kentucky fashion. Your letter informs me that your maiden name was Crume, and that you were raised in Washington county, Kentucky, by which I infer that an uncle of mine by marriage was a relative of yours. Nearly, or quite sixty years ago, Ralph Crume married Mary Lincoln, a sister of my father, in Washington county, Kentucky.

Accept my thanks, and believe me Very truly Your friend[.][13]

Letter of advice to Major General David Hunter, "Act well your part, there all the honor lies."

Lincoln makes a literary allusion to Alexander Pope.

Executive Mansion, Washington, Dec. 31, 1861

Dear Sir: Yours of the 23rd. is received; and I am constrained to say it is difficult to answer so ugly a letter in good temper. I am, as you intimate, losing much of the great confidence I placed in you, not from any act or omission of yours touching the public service, up to the time you were sent to Leavenworth, but from the flood of grumbling despatches and letters I have seen from you since. I knew you were being ordered to Leavenworth at the time it was done; and I aver that with as tender a regard for your honor and your sensibilities as I had for my own, it never occurred to me that you were being "humiliated, insulted and disgraced"; nor have I, up to this day, heard an intimation that you have been wronged, coming from any one but yourself. No one has blamed you for the retrograde movement from Springfield, nor for the information you gave Gen. Cameron; and this you could readily understand, if it were not for your unwarranted assumption that the ordering you to Leavenworth must necessarily have been done as a punishment for some fault. I thought then, and think yet, the position assigned to you is as respo[n]sible, and as honorable, as that assigned to Buell [at the time, a lower-ranking officer in the Union army]. I know that Gen. McClellan expected more important results from it. My impression is that at the time you were assigned to the new Western Department, it had not been determined to re-place Gen. Sherman in Kentucky; but of this I am not certain, because the idea that a command in Kentucky was very desireable, and one in the farther West, very undesireable, had never occurred to me. You constantly speak of being placed in command of only 3000. Now tell me, is not this mere impatience? Have you not known all the while that you are to command four or five times that many?

I have been, and am sincerely your friend; and if, as such, I dare to make a suggestion, I would say you are adopting the best possible way to ruin yourself. "Act well your part, there all the honor lies." He who does something at the head of one Regiment, will eclipse him who does nothing at the head of a hundred.[14]

Proclamation rescinding Major General David Hunter's order of military emancipation of May 9, 1862, "to declare the Slaves of any state or states, free . . . I reserve to myself . . ."

May 19, 1862

Whereas there appears in the public prints, what purports to be a proclamation, of Major General Hunter, in the words and figures following, towit:

Hilton Head, S.C., May 9, 1862.
General Orders No. 11.—The three States of Georgia, Florida and South Carolina, comprising the military department of the south, having deliberately declared themselves no longer under the protection of the United States of America, and having taken up arms against the said United States, it becomes a military

necessity to declare them under martial law. This was accordingly done on the
25th day of April, 1862. Slavery and martial law in a free country are altogether
incompatible; the persons in these three States—Georgia, Florida and South
Carolina—heretofore held as slaves, are therefore declared forever free. DAVID
HUNTER,
  (Official) Major General Commanding.
  ED. W. SMITH, Acting Assistant Adjutant General.

And whereas the same is producing some excitement, and misunderstanding: therefore

I, Abraham Lincoln, president of the United States, proclaim and declare, that the government of the United States, had no knowledge, information, or belief, of an intention on the part of General Hunter to issue such a proclamation; nor has it yet, any authentic information that the document is genuine. And further, that neither General Hunter, nor any other commander, or person, has been authorized by the Government of the United States, to make proclamations declaring the slaves of any State free; and that the supposed proclamation, now in question, whether genuine or false, is altogether void, so far as respects such declaration.

I further make known that whether it be competent for me, as Commander-in-Chief of the Army and Navy, to declare the Slaves of any state or states, free, and whether at any time, in any case, it shall have become a necessity indispensable to the maintainance of the government, to exercise such supposed power, are questions which, under my responsibility, I reserve to myself, and which I can not feel justified in leaving to the decision of commanders in the field. These are totally different questions from those of police regulations in armies and camps.

On the sixth day of March last, by a special message, I recommended to Congress the adoption of a joint resolution to be substantially as follows:

Resolved, That the United States ought to co-operate with any State which may adopt a gradual abolishment of slavery, giving to such State pecuniary aid, to be used by such State in its discretion to compensate for the inconveniences, public and private, produced by such change of system.

The resolution, in the language above quoted, was adopted by large majorities in both branches of Congress, and now stands an authentic, definite, and solemn proposal of the nation to the States and people most immediately interested in the subject matter. To the people of those states I now earnestly appeal. I do not argue. I beseech you to make the arguments for yourselves. You can not if you would, be blind to the signs of the times. I beg of you a calm and enlarged consideration of them, ranging, if it may be, far above personal and partizan politics. This proposal makes common cause for a common object, casting no reproaches upon any. It acts not the pharisee. The change it contemplates would come gently as the dews of heaven, not rending or wrecking anything. Will you not embrace it? So much good has not been done, by one effort, in all past time, as, in the providence of God, it is now your high previlege to do. May the vast future not have to lament that you have neglected it.[15]

15760

By May 1, 1862, when Lincoln wrote this note, his frustration with General George B. McClellan's inaction was beginning to show. "Parrott guns" were a ubiquitous artillery weapon used during the Civil War.

To General George B. McClellan, "hold all your ground . . ."

Washington City, D.C., June 1, 1862. 91/2 [A.M.]
Major Gen. McClellan

You are probably engaged with the enemy. I suppose he made the attack. Stand well on your guard—hold all your ground, or yield any only, inch by inch and in good order. This morning we merge Gen. Wool's department into yours, giving you command of the whole, and sending Gen. Dix to Fortress-Monroe, and Gen. Wool to Fort-McHenry. We also send Gen. Sigel to report to you for duty.[16]

To Benjamin F. Larned, paymaster general of the Army, "I shall be glad if you will kindly hear her, & do for her the best you can."

Executive Mansion, Washington, June 12, 1862
Pay-Master-General
My dear Sir:

The bearer of this, a french lady, so far as I can understand her, had a son in our volunteer Army, who was made a prisoner at Bull-Run, and has since died, at Mobile. He was only seventeen years of age; and she wishes, if possible, to draw what is due him, or some part of it. You will know, while I do not, whether this is possible. She is in great distress; and I shall be glad if you will kindly hear her, & do for her the best you can.[17]

Letter to Major General John C. Frémont, regarding the "fulfillment of understandings."

"Cypher"
Washington City, D.C., June 16, 1862
Major General Frémont
Mount Jackson, Va.

Your despatch of yesterday reminding me of a supposed understanding that I would furnish you a corps of thirty five thousand men, and asking of me "the fulfillment of this understanding" is received. I am ready to come to a fair settlement of accounts with you on the fulfillment of understandings.

Early in March last, when I assigned you to the command of the Mountain Department, I did tell you I would give you all the force I could, and that I hoped to make it reach thirty five thousand. You, at the same time told me that, within a reasonable time, you would seize the Railroad at, or East of, Knoxville, Tenn. if you could. There was then in the Department a force supposed to be twentyfive thousand—the exact number as well known to you as to me. After looking about two or three days you called and distinctly told me that if I would add the Blecker [Blenker] Division to the force already in the Department, you would undertake the job. The Blecker [Blenker] division contained ten thousand; and at the expense of great dissatisfaction to Gen. McClellan, I took it from his army, and gave it to you. My promise was litterally fulfilled. I had given you all I could, and I had given you very nearly if not quite thirtyfive thousand.

Now for yours. On the 23rd. of May, largely over two months afterwards, you were at Franklin Va, not within three hundred miles of Knoxville, nor within eighty miles of any part of the Railroad East of it—and not moving forward, but telegraphing here that you could not move for lack of everything. Now, do not misunderstand me. I do not say you have not done all you could. I presume you met unexpected difficulties; and I beg you to believe that as surely as you have done your best, so have I. I have not the power now to fill up your corps to thirtyfive thousand. I am not demanding of you to do the work of thirtyfive thousand. I am only asking of you to stand cautiously on the defensive, get your force in order, and give such protection as you can to the valley of the Shenandoah, and to Western Virginia. Have you received the orders? and will you act upon them?[18]

Memorandum on recruiting negroes, "to carrying away slaves not suitable for recruits, objection."

[July 22, 1862?]

To recruiting free negroes, no objection.

To recruiting slaves of disloyal owners, no objection.

To recruiting slaves of loyal owners, with their consent, no objection.

To recruiting slaves of loyal owners without consent, objection, unless the necessity is urgent.

To conducting offensively, while recruiting, and to carrying away slaves not suitable for recruits, objection.[19]

Private letter to Reverdy Johnson, "I shall not surrender this game leaving any available card unplayed."

Reverdy Johnson was an emissary sent by Lincoln to investigate and review decisions by the military tribunal in the Union-occupied city of New Orleans.

July 26, 1862

It seems the Union feeling in Louisiana is being crushed out by the course of General Phelps. Please pardon me for believing that is a false pretense. The people of Louisiana—all intelligent people every where—know full well, that I never had a wish to touch the foundations of their society, or any right of theirs. With perfect knowledge of this, they forced a necessity upon me to send armies among them, and it is their own fault, not mine, that they are annoyed by the presence of General Phelps. They also know the remedy—know how to be cured of General Phelps. Remove the necessity of his presence. And might it not be well for them to consider whether they have not already had time enough to do this?

If they can conceive of anything worse than General Phelps, within my power, would they not better be looking out for it? They very well know the way to avert all this is simply to take their place in the Union upon the old terms. If they will not do this, should they not receive harder blows rather than lighter ones?

You are ready to say I apply to friends what is due only to enemies. I distrust the wisdom if not the sincerity of friends, who would hold my hands while my enemies stab me. This appeal of professed friends has paralyzed me more in this struggle than any other one thing. You remember telling me the day after the Baltimore mob in April 1861, that it would crush all Union feeling in Maryland for me to attempt bringing troops over Maryland soil to Washington. I brought the troops notwithstanding, and yet there was Union feeling enough left to elect a Legislature the next autumn which in turn elected a very excellent Union U. S. Senator!

I am a patient man—always willing to forgive on the Christian terms of repentance; and also to give ample time for repentance. Still I must save this government if possible. What I cannot do, of course I will not do; but it may as well be understood, once for all, that I shall not surrender this game leaving any available card unplayed.[20]

Address on colonization to a delegation of free blacks, "I want you to let me know whether this can be done or not."

August 14, 1862

Perhaps you have long been free, or all your lives. Your race are suffering, in my judgment, the greatest wrong inflicted on any people. But even when you cease to be slaves, you are yet far removed from being placed on an equality with the white race. You are cut off from many of the advantages which the other race enjoy. The aspiration of men is to enjoy equality with the best when free, but on this broad continent, not a single man of your race is made the equal of a single man of ours. Go where you are treated the best, and the ban is still upon you.

. . . I need not recount to you the effects upon white men, growing out of the institution of Slavery. I believe in its general evil effects on the white race. See our present condition—the country engaged in war!—our white men cutting one another's throats, none knowing how far it will extend; and then consider what we know to be the truth. But for your race among us there could not be war, although many men engaged on either side do not care for you one way or the other. Nevertheless, I repeat, without the institution of Slavery and the colored race as a basis, the war could not have an existence.

It is better for us both, therefore, to be separated. I know that there are free men among you, who even if they could better their condition are not as much inclined to go out of the country as those, who being slaves could obtain their freedom on this condition. I suppose one of the principal difficulties in the way of colonization is that the free colored man cannot see that his comfort would be advanced by it. You may believe you can live in Washington or elsewhere in the United States the remainder of your life [as easily], perhaps more so than you can in any foreign country, and hence you may come to the conclusion that you have nothing to do with the idea of going to a foreign country. This is (I speak in no unkind sense) an extremely selfish view of the case.

The question is if the colored people are persuaded to go anywhere, why not [Liberia]? One reason for an unwillingness to do so is that some of you would rather remain within reach of the country of your nativity. I do not know how much attachment you may have toward our race. It does not strike me that you have the greatest reason to love them. But still you are attached to them at all events.

The place I am thinking about having for a colony is in Central America. It is nearer to us than Liberia—not much more than one-fourth as far as Liberia, and within seven days' run by steamers. Unlike Liberia it is on a great line of travel—it is a highway. The country is a very excellent one for any people, and with great natural resources and advantages, and especially because of the similarity of climate with your native land—thus being suited to your physical condition.

The particular place I have in view is to be a great highway from the Atlantic or Caribbean Sea to the Pacific Ocean, and this particular place has all the advantages for a colony. On both sides there are harbors among the finest in the world. Again, there is evidence of very rich coal mines. A certain amount of coal is valuable in any country, and there may be more than enough for the wants of the country. Why I attach so much importance to coal is, it will afford an opportunity to the inhabitants for immediate employment till they get ready to settle permanently in their homes.

If you take colonists where there is no good landing, there is a bad show; and so where there is nothing to cultivate, and of which to make a farm. But if something is started so that you can get your daily bread as soon as you reach there, it is a great advantage. Coal land is the best thing I know of with which to commence an enterprise.

. . . I want you to let me know whether this can be done or not. This is the practical part of my wish to see you. These are subjects of very great importance, worthy of a month's study, [instead] of a speech delivered in an hour. I ask you then to consider seriously not pertaining to yourselves merely, nor for your race, and ours, for the present time, but as one of the things, if successfully managed, for the good of mankind—not confined to the present generation, but as

"From age to age descends the lay,
To millions yet to be,
Till far its echoes roll away,
Into eternity."[21]

Letter to Horace Greeley, "If I could save the Union without freeing any slave I would do it . . ."

Horace Greeley, a leading abolitionist, was the influential publisher of the New-York Tribune. *Lincoln wrote this letter in response to an open letter to the president published in the newspaper not long before. Lincoln had already drafted the preliminary Emancipation Proclamation when writing this letter, and was to issue it exactly a month later.*

Washington, August 22, 1862

. . . If there be in [your letter] any statements, or assumptions of fact, which I may know to be erroneous, I do not, now and here, controvert them. If there be in it any inferences which I may believe to be falsely drawn, I do not now and here, argue against them. If there be perceptible in it an impatient and dictatorial tone, I waive it in deference to an old friend, whose heart I have always supposed to be right.

As to the policy I "seem to be pursuing" as you say, I have not meant to leave any one in doubt.

I would save the Union. I would save it the shortest way under the Constitution. The sooner the national authority can be restored; the nearer the Union will be "the Union as it was." If there be those who would not save the Union, unless they could at the same time save slavery, I do not agree with them. If there be those who would not save the Union unless they could at the same time destroy slavery, I do not agree with them. My paramount object in this struggle is to save the Union, and is not either to save or to destroy slavery. If I could save the Union without freeing any slave I would do it, and if I could save it by freeing all the slaves I would do it; and if I could save it by freeing some and leaving others alone I would also do that. What I do about slavery, and the colored race, I do because I believe it helps to save the Union; and what I forbear, I forbear because I do not believe it would help to save the Union. I shall do less whenever I shall believe what I am doing hurts the cause, and I shall do more whenever I shall believe doing more will help the cause. I shall try to correct errors when shown to be errors; and I shall adopt new views so fast as they shall appear to be true views.

I have here stated my purpose according to my view of official duty; and I intend no modification of my oft-expressed personal wish that all men every where could be free.[22]

Portrait of Horace Greeley (1811–1872), taken ca. 1855–1865. Greeley had a testy relationship with Lincoln. Born in New England, Greeley moved to New York in 1831, where he quickly established himself as a journalist and as a leader of the antislavery movement. Greeley founded the *New-York Tribune* in 1841, and developed it into an influential newspaper with the highest circulation in the United States. After helping to found the Republican party in 1854, he continually pushed the party toward an uncompromising abolitionist stance, which brought him into frequent conflict with Lincoln, whom he considered too conciliatory to the South and too accepting of slavery where it already existed. Greeley opposed Lincoln's renomination in 1864, and unsuccessfully ran for president against Ulysses S. Grant in 1872.

4. "Thenceforward, and Forever Free"

This portrait of a sleepy-eyed Lincoln was taken by the photographer Lewis Walker in 1863.

On the recommendation of Secretary of State William Seward, Lincoln waited until the Union scored a military victory—which came at Antietam on September 17, 1862—before issuing the preliminary Emancipation Proclamation (p. 151) on September 22, 1862, in order to avoid the perception that it was a politically desperate act. According to the Proclamation, slaves in any state still in rebellion against the Union on January 1, 1863, would be "then, thenceforward, and forever free." Lincoln had done what he had repeatedly said he had no mandate to do or interest in doing: beyond simply preventing the expansion of slavery, he would permanently ban it where it legally existed in slave-holding states. For the first time, millions of legally enslaved people in the United States would be slaves no more—unless the rebel state where he or she happened to live agreed to rejoin the Union. When rebel states failed to do so, Lincoln, as promised, issued the final Emancipation Proclamation on New Year's Day in 1863, and roughly three million slaves became free in the eyes of the United States government.

The Proclamation had an almost instantaneous and profound effect on the population, black and white, North and South, Union and Confederate. Slaves in slave states in which the Union army had taken control were immediately freed. Tens of thousands of slaves who were near Union lines made a dash for freedom. Runaways who had been held in Union camps as "war contraband" were released. As the Union army advanced, slaves in the areas where the rebellion was quelled became free as well.

The flow of freed and escaped slaves to Union-controlled areas had the practical result of damaging the Confederate economy and removing a vital support element of the Confederate war machine, as enslaved cooks, mechanics, and farm and factory workers were lost. Moreover, the Emancipation Proclamation all but eliminated the threat that France and Great Britain, which had already abolished slavery, would support the Confederate war effort or recognize the Confederate government.

Aware that the Proclamation was on dubious constitutional grounds, Lincoln was careful to couch it as a wartime act, performed out of military necessity. When Secretary of the Treasury Salmon Chase expressed frustration that certain areas of Virginia and Louisiana were exempted from the final Proclamation, Lincoln replied, "without the argument of military necessity, and so, without any argument, except the one that I think the measure politically expedient, and morally right? Would I not thus give up all footing upon constitution or law? Would I not thus be in the boundless field of absolutism?"

The Proclamation had the additional effect of swelling the ranks of the Union army—Lincoln added a call for the recruitment of black soldiers to the final Proclamation that had not been in the preliminary version. In March 1863, Lincoln wrote to Andrew Johnson, the military governor of Tennessee, a Union loyalist who was a slave holder, "The bare sight of fifty thousand armed, and drilled black soldiers on the banks of the Mississippi, would end the rebellion at once." Johnson became Lincoln's vice president in his second term, ascending to the presidency after Lincoln's assassination.

Suddenly faced with a population of freed black people in the United States, and having abandoned the idea of colonization, Lincoln was faced with the question of what to do with a free black population. Would they be citizens? Something less than citizens? The first hint as to how Lincoln might handle this question came in his very gingerly worded letter to Michael Hahn, the governor of free-state Louisiana (p. 191). "I barely suggest for your private consideration," Lincoln wrote, "whether some of the colored people may not be let in [to the elective franchise]—as, for instance, the very intelligent, and especially those who have fought gallantly in our ranks." It is interesting to contemplate how differently Reconstruction might have been carried out had Lincoln survived.

∽ゥ

Lincoln became increasingly involved in the war effort and was known to spend long nights in the White House telegraph office, hungrily taking in news of the war and disseminating orders. His frustration with the slow pace of the war, particularly the inaction of the commander of the Union armies, George McClellan, began to boil over. In October 1862, he chided McClellan for his overcautiousness, even daring to suggest where and how he might engage the enemy (p. 155). He needled McClellan for offering excuses rather than taking action—in one instance, fatigued horses. "Will you pardon me for asking what the horses of your army have done since the battle of Antietam that fatigue anything," Lincoln pointedly asked him (p. 157). McClellan, who had privately been disparaging Lincoln, was to be his Democratic opponent in the presidential election of 1864.

Relieved as Lincoln was to have Ulysses S. Grant emerge as the implacable military leader he needed ("you were right, and I was wrong," he effusively wrote to Grant after a Union victory), polite vexation characterized his

Lincoln meets with General
George B. McClellan in the
general's tent at Antietam,
Maryland, after the battle there.
Alexander Gardner made this
photograph on October 3, 1862.
While Lincoln was slowly losing
his patience with McClellan, the
general was privately ridiculing
the commander-in-chief to friends
and allies. Lincoln replaced
McClellan as the commander of
the Army of the Potomac with
Major General Ambrose Burnside
on November 5, 1862. In 1864,
McClellan was the Democratic
party's nominee for president.
Lincoln defeated him handily,
winning a sizable majority of the
vote among active military and
veterans.

communication to most of his generals. There is no better example of this than his unsent letter to General George G. Meade (p. 174), who had let Robert E. Lee escape southward after defeating him at Gettysburg: "I do not believe you appreciate the magnitude of the misfortune involved in Lee's escape," wrote Lincoln. "He was within your easy grasp, and to have closed upon him would, in connection with our other late successes, have ended the war. As it is, the war will be prolonged indefinitely."

As the war ground on, Lincoln became increasingly philosophical, deeply pondering the metaphysical questions he had jotted down in his "Meditation on the Divine Will" in 1862. At the dedication of the Gettysburg cemetery in November 1863 (p. 188), Lincoln drew on these ideas, poetically imbuing the epic struggle and the unimaginable loss of life at Gettysburg and the war in general with moral, religious, and historical meaning. That he did so in 272 words and two minutes, almost as an afterthought following a two-hour speech

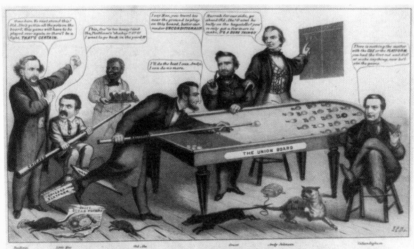

A LITTLE GAME OF BAGATELLE, BETWEEN OLD ABE THE RAIL SPLITTER & LITTLE MAC THE GUNBOAT GENERAL.

This cartoon, published in a Philadelphia newspaper in 1864 during the presidential campaign, presents the race between Lincoln (shooting with a cue marked "Baltimore," the site of the Republican convention) and the Democratic candidate, George B. McClellan (seated, second from left, holding a cue labeled with the site of the Democratic convention), as a game of bagatelle, a popular nineteenth-century game derived from billiards.

by the featured speaker, the eminent lecturer Edward Everett, is a testament to Lincoln's genius as a writer.

Lincoln's second inaugural address, rife with biblical allusions (p. 206), was principally an attempt at conciliation with the defeated South: "with malice toward none, and charity for all." Yet along with the olive branch, using the cadences and themes of a religious sermon, Lincoln made his moral judgment clear: the nation's struggles in the war had been God's retribution for the sin of slavery.

With two months left in the 1864 campaign, Lincoln expected to be defeated for a second term, and wrote a fatalistic memo to his cabinet to that effect on August 23, 1864 (see p. 197). But after a series of Union military victories— Lincoln was closely involved in military affairs until the war's end—he handily defeated his Democratic opponent, none other than General George B. McClellan, the "over-cautious" thorn in Lincoln's side through the years of the Civil War.

Lincoln spent the final months of his life laying the groundwork for Reconstruction, enacting the conciliatory policies that he had promised in his first inaugural address, but giving no quarter on the issue of slavery. He acted to solidify the rights granted in the Emancipation Proclamation by feverishly working to obtain congressional approval of a constitutional amendment abolishing slavery. On January 13, 1865, against long odds, two-thirds of the House of Representatives approved a resolution to submit the amendment to the states for ratification, with a margin of victory of three votes. An earlier vote had ended in defeat.

On April 9, 1865, General Robert E. Lee surrendered to Ulysses S. Grant at Appomattox House, Virginia. Five days later, after presiding over a cabinet meeting, Lincoln left the White House with Mary to attend a production of *Our American Cousin* at Ford's Theatre, where the well-known actor and Southern sympathizer John Wilkes Booth later entered.

Lincoln died early the next morning. The Thirteenth Amendment to the U.S. Constitution was ratified on December 6, 1865, nearly eight months after his death.

The will of God prevails— In great contests
each party claims to act in accordance with
the will of God. Both may be, and one
must be wrong. God can not be for, and
against the same thing at the same time.
In the present civil war it is quite possible
that God's purpose is something different from
the purpose of either party— and yet the human
instrumentalities, working just as they do, are of
the best adaptation to effect His purpose. I am
almost ready to say this is probably true— that
God wills this contest, and wills that it shall
not end yet— By his mere quiet power, on the minds
of the now contestants, He could have either saved
or destroyed the Union without a human contest— Yet the contest began— And having begun
He could give the final victory to either side
any day— Yet the contest proceeds—

In the midst of his management of the military conduct of the Civil War, and the quotidian business of the presidency, Lincoln took the time to write a ruminative note to himself about God's will in the present conflict. One can see the spiritual under-pinnings of the Gettysburg Address and his second inaugural address taking shape.

Meditation on the Divine Will, "God can not be for, and against the same thing at the same time."

This is the text of a private note written by Lincoln during the period leading up to the issuing of the preliminary Emancipation Proclamation.

[September 2, 1862?]

The will of God prevails. In great contests each party claims to act in accordance with the will of God. Both may be, and one must be wrong. God can not be for, and against the same thing at the same time. In the present civil war it is quite possible that God's purpose is something different from the purpose of either party—and yet the human instrumentalities, working just as they do, are of the best adaptation to effect His purpose. I am almost ready to say this is probably true—that God wills this contest, and wills that it shall not end yet. By his mere quiet power, on the minds of the now contestants, He could have either saved or destroyed the Union without a human contest. Yet the contest began. And having begun He could give the final victory to either side any day. Yet the contest proceeds.[1]

Preliminary Emancipation Proclamation, "all persons held as slaves within any state, or designated part of a state, the people whereof shall then be in rebellion against the United States shall be then, thenceforward, and forever free."

September 22, 1862
By the President of the
United States of America
A Proclamation.

I, Abraham Lincoln, President of the United States of America, and Commander-in-chief of the Army and Navy thereof, do hereby proclaim and declare that hereafter, as heretofore, the war will be prossecuted for the object of practically restoring the constitutional relation between the United States, and each of the

This page of Lincoln's original draft of the preliminary Emancipation Proclamation shows where he pasted in the recently passed acts of Congress that he used, in part, to justify the issuing of the edict. The acts centered on the seizure of private property in order to punish and suppress rebellion. Lincoln's reasoning did not prevent outcries of tyranny from his critics—nor did it offer relief to slaves held in areas that were controlled by Union forces or that were not actively engaged in revolt.

states, and the people thereof, in which states that relation is, or may be suspended, or disturbed.

That it is my purpose, upon the next meeting of Congress to again recommend the adoption of a practical measure tendering pecuniary aid to the free acceptance or rejection of all slave-states, so called, the people whereof may not then be in rebellion against the United States, and which states, may then have voluntarily adopted, or thereafter may voluntarily adopt, immediate, or gradual abolishment of slavery within their respective limits; and that the effort to colonize persons of African descent, with their consent, upon this continent, or elsewhere, with the previously obtained consent of the Governments existing there, will be continued.

That on the first day of January in the year of our Lord, one thousand eight hundred and sixty-three, all persons held as slaves within any state, or designated part of a state, the people whereof shall then be in rebellion against the United States shall be then, thenceforward, and forever free; and the executive government of the United States, including the military and naval authority thereof, will recognize and maintain the freedom of such persons, and will do no act or acts to repress such persons, or any of them, in any efforts they may make for their actual freedom.

That the executive will, on the first day of January aforesaid, by proclamation, designate the States, and parts of states, if any, in which the people thereof respectively, shall then be in rebellion against the United States; and the fact that any state, or the people thereof shall, on that day be, in good faith represented in the Congress of the United States, by members chosen thereto, at elections wherein a majority of the qualified voters of such state shall have participated, shall, in the absence of strong countervailing testimony, be deemed conclusive evidence that such state and the people thereof, are not then in rebellion against the United States.[2]

Testimonial for Isachar Zacharie, Lincoln's chiropodist

Lincoln had a close relationship with Zacharie, and in 1865 would intervene with Secretary of War Stanton to allow Zacharie to bring members of his family north from Savannah (see p. 202).

Sep. 22, 1862

Dr. Zacharie has operated on my feet with great success, and considerable addition to my comfort.[3]

Reply to serenaders, "I suppose it is because of the proclamation."

Over the course of his presidency, groups occasionally assembled on the White House lawn to serenade Lincoln and he would sometimes return the favor by speaking to them from the windows of the second floor.

September 24, 1862

Fellow citizens: I appear before you to do little more than acknowledge the courtesy you pay me, and to thank you for it. I have not been distinctly informed why it is this occasion you appear to do me this honor, though I suppose [interruptions] it is because of the proclamation. [Cries of "Good," and applause.] I was about to say, I suppose I understand it. [Laughter—Voices: "That you do," "You thoroughly understand it."] What I did, I did after very full deliberation, and under a very heavy and solemn sense of responsibility. [Cries of "Good," "Good," "Bless you," and applause.]

I can only trust in God I have made no mistake. [Cries of "No mistake—all right; you've made no mistakes yet. Go ahead, you're right."] I shall make no attempt on this occasion to sustain what I have done or said by any comment.

[Voices—"That's unnecessary; we understand it."] It is now for the country and the world to pass judgment on it, and, may be, take action upon it. I will say no more upon this subject. In my position I am environed with difficulties. [A voice—"That's so."]

Yet they are scarcely so great as the difficulties of those who, upon the battle field, are endeavoring to purchase with their blood and their lives the future happiness and prosperity of this country. [Applause, long and continued.] Let us never forget them. On the 14th and 17th days of the present month there have been battles bravely, skillfully and successfully fought. [Applause.] We do not yet know the particulars. Let us be sure that in giving praise to particular individuals, we do no injustice to others. I only ask you, at the conclusion of these few remarks, to give three hearty cheers to all good and brave officers and men who fought those successful battles.

Proclamation suspending the writ of habeas corpus

September 24, 1862
By the President of the United States of America:
A Proclamation.

Whereas, it has become necessary to call into service not only volunteers but also portions of the militia of the States by draft in order to suppress the insurrection existing in the United States, and disloyal persons are not adequately restrained by the ordinary processes of law from hindering this measure and from giving aid and comfort in various ways to the insurrection;

Now, therefore, be it ordered, first, that during the existing insurrection and as a necessary measure for suppressing the same, all Rebels and Insurgents, their aiders and abettors within the United States, and all persons discouraging volunteer enlistments, resisting militia drafts, or guilty of any disloyal practice, affording aid and comfort to Rebels against the authority of the United States, shall be subject to martial law and liable to trial and punishment by Courts Martial or Military Commission:

Lincoln with General George B. McClellan and his staff at Antietam in October 1862. "Little Mac" stands directly opposite the President; Lincoln calmly rests his hand on a chair; the figure at the far right in the tall hat holding a cavalry sword is Captain George Armstrong Custer.

Second. That the Writ of Habeas Corpus is suspended in respect to all persons arrested, or who are now, or hereafter during the rebellion shall be, imprisoned in any fort, camp, arsenal, military prison, or other place of confinement by any military authority or by the sentence of any Court Martial or Military Commission.

In witness whereof, I have hereunto set my hand, and caused the seal of the United States to be affixed.

[L.S.]

Done at the City of Washington this twenty fourth day of September, in the year of our Lord one thousand eight hundred and sixty-two, and of the Independence of the United States the 87th.[4]

Letter to Major General George B. McClellan, "Are you not over-cautious when you assume that you can not do what the enemy is constantly doing?"

Lincoln chides McClellan for his inaction and suggests a detailed military strategy.

Executive Mansion, Washington, Oct. 13, 1862.
My dear Sir

You remember my speaking to you of what I called your over-cautiousness. Are you not over-cautious when you assume that you can not do what the enemy is constantly doing? Should you not claim to be at least his equal in prowess, and act upon the claim?

As I understand, you telegraph Gen. Halleck that you can not subsist your army at Winchester unless the Railroad from Harper's Ferry to that point be put in working order. But the enemy does now subsist his army at Winchester at a distance nearly twice as great from railroad transportation as you would have to do without the railroad last named. He now wagons from Culpepper C.H. [Court House] which is just about twice as far as you would have to do from Harper's Ferry. He is certainly not more than half as well provided with wagons as you are. I certainly should be pleased for you to have the advantage of the Railroad from Harper's Ferry to Winchester, but it wastes all the remainder of autumn to give it to you; and, in fact ignores the question of time, which can not, and must not be ignored.

Again, one of the standard maxims of war, as you know, is "to operate upon the enemy's communications as much as possible without exposing your own." You seem to act as if this applies against you, but can not apply in your favor. Change positions with the enemy, and think you not he would break your communication with Richmond within the next twentyfour hours? You dread his going into Pennsylvania. But if he does so in full force, he gives up his communications to you absolutely, and you have nothing to do but to follow, and ruin him; if he does so with less than full force, fall upon, and beat what is left behind all the easier.

Exclusive of the water line, you are now nearer Richmond than the enemy is by the route that you can, and he must take. Why can you not reach there before him, unless you admit that he is more than your equal on a march. His route is the arc of a circle, while yours is the chord. The roads are as good on yours as on his.

You know I desired, but did not order, you to cross the Potomac below, instead of above the Shenandoah and Blue Ridge. My idea was that this would at once menace the enemies' communications, which I would seize if he would permit. If he should move Northward I would follow him closely, holding his communications. If he should prevent our seizing his communications, and move towards Richmond, I would press closely to him, fight him if a favorable opportunity should present, and, at least, try to beat him to Richmond on the inside track. I say "try"; if we never try, we shall never succeed. If he make a stand at Winchester, moving neither North or South, I would fight him there, on the idea that if we can not beat him when he bears the wastage of coming to us, we never can when we bear the wastage of going to him. This proposition is a simple truth, and is too important to be lost sight of for a moment. In coming to us, he tenders us an advantage which we should not waive. We should not so operate as to merely drive him away. As we must beat him somewhere, or fail finally, we can do it, if at all, easier near to us, than far away. If we can not beat the enemy where he now is, we never can, he again being within the entrenchments of Richmond.

Recurring to the idea of going to Richmond on the inside track, the facility of supplying from the side away from the enemy is remarkable—as it were, by the different spokes of a wheel extending from the hub towards the rim—and this whether you move directly by the chord, or on the inside arc, hugging the Blue Ridge more closely. The chord-line, as you see, carries you by Aldie, Hay-Market, and Fredericksburg; and you see how turn-pikes, railroads, and finally, the Potomac by Acquia Creek, meet you at all points from Washington. The same, only the lines lengthened a little, if you press closer to the Blue Ridge part of the way. The gaps through the Blue Ridge I understand to be about the following distances from Harper's Ferry, towit: Vestal's five miles; Gregorie's, thirteen, Snicker's eighteen, Ashby's, twenty-eight, Mannassas, thirty-eight, Chester fortyfive, and Thornton's fiftythree. I should think it preferable to take the route nearest the enemy, disabling him to make an important move without your knowledge, and compelling him to keep his forces together, for dread of you. The gaps would enable you to attack if you should wish. For a great part of the way, you would be practically between the enemy and both Washington and Richmond, enabling us to spare you the greatest number of troops from here. When at length, running for Richmond ahead of him enables him to move this way; if he does so, turn and attack him in rear. But I think he should be engaged long before such point is reached. It is all easy if our troops march as well as the enemy; and it is unmanly to say they can not do it.

This letter is in no sense an order.[5]

Telegram to George B. McClellan, "Will you pardon me for asking . . ."

Lincoln loses his patience, but with customary humor.

Washington City, D.C., Oct. 24 [25], 1862
Majr. Genl. McClellan

I have just read your despatch about sore tongued and fatiegued horses. Will you pardon me for asking what the horses of your army have done since the battle of Antietam that fatigue anything?[6]

Washington City. D.C.

Oct 24. 1862

Major Genl McClellan

I have just read your despatch about sore tongued and fatiegued horses — Will you pardon me for asking what the horses of your army have done since the battle of Antietam that fatigue anything?

A. Lincoln

Lincoln's note to General George B. McClellan, sent October 24, 1862: "pardon me for asking what the horses of your army have done since the battle of Antietam that fatigue anything?"

Annual Message to Congress, December 1, 1862, "The fiery trial through which we pass, will light us down, in honor or dishonor . . ."

Lincoln proposes constitutional amendments granting gradual compensated emancipation and appropriating funds for the colonization of free blacks outside the United States.

Fellow-citizens of the Senate and House of Representatives:

Since your last annual assembling another year of health and bountiful harvests has passed. And while it has not pleased the Almighty to bless us with a return of peace, we can but press on, guided by the best light He gives us, trusting that in His own good time, and wise way, all will yet be well.

. . . On the twenty-second day of September last a proclamation was issued by the Executive, a copy of which is herewith submitted.

In accordance with the purpose expressed in the second paragraph of that paper, I now respectfully recall your attention to what may be called "compensated emancipation."

A nation may be said to consist of its territory, its people, and its laws. The territory is the only part which is of certain durability. "One generation passeth away, and another generation cometh, but the earth abideth forever." It is of the first importance to duly consider, and estimate, this ever-enduring part. That portion of the earth's surface which is owned and inhabited by the people of the United States, is well adapted to be the home of one national family; and it is not well adapted for two, or more. Its vast extent, and its variety of climate and productions, are of advantage, in this age, for one people, whatever they might have been in former ages. Steam, telegraphs, and intelligence, have brought these, to be an advantageous combination, for one united people.

. . . There is no line, straight or crooked, suitable for a national boundary, upon which to divide. Trace through, from east to west, upon the line between the free and slave country, and we shall find a little more than one-third of its length are rivers, easy to be crossed, and populated, or soon to be populated, thickly upon both sides; while nearly all its remaining length, are merely surveyor's lines, over which people may walk back and forth without any consciousness of their presence. No part of this line can be made any more difficult to pass, by writing it down on paper, or parchment, as a national boundary. The fact of separation, if it comes, gives up, on the part of the seceding section, the fugitive slave clause, along with all other constitutional obligations upon the section seceded from, while I should expect no treaty stipulation would ever be made to take its place.

But there is another difficulty. The great interior region, bounded east by the Alleghanies, north by the British dominions, west by the Rocky mountains, and south by the line along which the culture of corn and cotton meets, and which includes part of Virginia, part of Tennessee, all of Kentucky, Ohio, Indiana, Michigan, Wisconsin, Illinois, Missouri, Kansas, Iowa, Minnesota and the Territories of Dakota, Nebraska, and part of Colorado, already has above ten millions of people, and will have fifty millions within fifty years, if not prevented by any political folly or mistake. It contains more than one-third of the country owned by the United States—certainly more than one million of square miles. Once half as populous as Massachusetts already is, it would have more than seventy-five millions of people. A glance at the map shows that, territorially speaking, it is the great body of the republic. The other parts are but marginal borders to it, the magnificent region sloping west from the rocky mountains to the Pacific, being the deepest, and also the richest, in undeveloped resources. In the production of provisions, grains, grasses, and all which proceed from them, this great interior region is naturally one of the most important in the world. Ascertain from the statistics the small proportion of the region which has, as yet, been brought into cultivation, and also the large and rapidly increasing amount of its products, and we shall be overwhelmed with the magnitude of the prospect presented. An[d] yet this region has no sea-coast, touches no ocean anywhere. As part of one nation, its people now find, and may forever find, their way to Europe by New York, to South America and Africa by New Orleans, and to Asia by San Francisco. But separate our common country into two nations, as designed by the present rebellion, and every man of this great interior region is thereby cut off from some one or more of these outlets, not, perhaps, by a physical barrier, but by embarrassing and onerous trade regulations.

. . . "Resolved by the Senate and House of Representatives of the United States of America in Congress assembled, (two thirds of both houses concurring,) That the following articles be proposed to the legislatures (or conventions) of the several States as amendments to the Constitution of the United States, all or any of which articles when ratified by three-fourths of the said legislatures (or conventions) to be valid as part or parts of the said Constitution, viz:

"Article —.

"Every State, wherein slavery now exists, which shall abolish the same therein, at any time, or times, before the first day of January, in the year of our Lord one thousand and nine hundred, shall receive compensation from the United States as follows, to wit:

"The President of the United States shall deliver to every such State, bonds of the United States, bearing interest at the rate of _ per cent, per annum, to an amount equal to the aggregate sum of _ for each slave shown to have been therein, by the eig[h]th census of the United States, said bonds to be delivered to such State by instalments, or in one parcel, at the completion of the abolishment, accordingly as the same shall have been gradual, or at one time, within such State; and interest shall begin to run upon any such bond, only from the proper time of its delivery as aforesaid. Any State having received bonds as aforesaid, and afterwards reintroducing or tolerating slavery therein, shall refund to the United States the bonds so received, or the value thereof, and all interest paid thereon.

"Article —.

"All slaves who shall have enjoyed actual freedom by the chances of the war, at any time before the end of the rebellion, shall be forever free; but all owners of such, who shall not have been disloyal, shall be compensated for them, at the same rates as is provided for States adopting abolishment of slavery, but in such way, that no slave shall be twice accounted for.

"Article —.

"Congress may appropriate money, and otherwise provide, for colonizing free colored persons, with their own consent, at any place or places without the United States."

The emancipation will be unsatisfactory to the advocates of perpetual slavery; but the length of time should greatly mitigate their dissatisfaction. The time spares both races from the evils of sudden derangement—in fact, from the necessity of any derangement—while most of those whose habitual course of thought will be disturbed by the measure will have passed away before its consummation. They will never see it. Another class will hail the prospect of emancipation, but will deprecate the length of time. They will feel that it gives too little to the now living slaves. But it really gives them much. It saves them from the vagrant destitution which must largely attend immediate emancipation in localities where their numbers are very great; and it gives the inspiring assurance that their posterity shall be free forever. The plan leaves to each State, choosing to act under it, to abolish slavery now, or at the end of the century, or at any intermediate time, or by degrees, extending over the whole or any part of the period; and it obliges no two states to proceed alike. It also provides for compensation, and generally the mode of making it. This, it would seem, must further mitigate the dissatisfaction of those who favor perpetual slavery, and especially of those who are to receive the compensation. Doubtless some of those who are to pay, and not to receive will object. Yet the measure is both just and economical. In a certain sense the liberation of slaves is the destruction of property—property acquired by descent, or by purchased, the same as any other property. It is no less true for having been often said, that the people of the south are not more responsible for the original introduction of this property, than are the people of the north; and when it is remembered how unhesitatingly we all use cotton and sugar, and share the profits of dealing in them, it may not be quite safe to say, that the south has been more responsible than the north for its continuance. If then, for a common object, this property is to be sacrificed is it not just that it be done at a common charge?

... It is insisted that their presence would injure, and displace white labor and white laborers. If there ever could be a proper time for mere catch arguments, that time surely is not now. In times like the present, men should utter nothing for which they would not willingly be responsible through time and in eternity. Is it true, then, that colored people can displace any more white labor, by being free, than by remaining slaves? If they stay in their old places, they jostle no white laborers; if they leave their old places, they leave them open to white laborers. Logically, there is neither more nor less of it. Emancipation, even without deportation, would probably enhance the wages of white labor, and, very surely, would not reduce them.

... Fellow-citizens, we cannot escape history. We of this Congress and this administration, will be remembered in spite of ourselves. No personal significance, or insignificance, can spare one or another of us. The fiery trial through which we pass, will light us down, in honor or dishonor, to the latest generation. We say we are for the Union. The world will not forget that we say this. We know how to save the Union. The world knows we do know how to save it. We—even we here—hold the power, and bear the responsibility. In giving freedom to the slave, we assure freedom to the free—honorable alike in what we give, and what we preserve. We shall nobly save, or meanly lose, the last best, hope of earth. Other means may succeed; this could not fail. The way is plain, peaceful, generous, just—a way which, if followed, the world will forever applaud, and God must forever bless.[7]

Letter to Major General Samuel R. Curtis, "restore the old man to his home . . ."

Requesting that Nathaniel W. Watkins, a former political ally from Missouri to whom Lincoln had extended amnesty after Watkins renounced his Confederate ties and declared loyalty to the Union, be allowed to return to his house.

St. Louis, Mo., Dec. 16, 1862

N. W. Watkins, of Jackson, Mo. (who is half brother to Henry Clay) writes me that a Col. of ours has driven him from his home at Jackson. Will you please look into the case, and restore the old man to his home, if the public interest will admit?[8]

Condolence letter to Fanny McCullough, "to the young, it comes with bitterest agony, because it takes them unawares."

Fanny McCullough was the daughter of Lieutenant Colonel William McCullough, Lincoln's friend and colleague from his days on the McClean County Illinois legal circuit. William McCullough was killed in battle in Mississippi on December 5, 1862.

Executive Mansion, Washington, December 23, 1862
Dear Fanny

It is with deep grief that I learn of the death of your kind and brave Father; and, especially, that it is affecting your young heart beyond what is common in such cases. In this sad world of ours, sorrow comes to all; and, to the young, it comes with bitterest agony, because it takes them unawares. The older have learned to ever expect it. I am anxious to afford some alleviation of your present distress. Perfect relief is not possible, except with time. You can not now realize that you will ever feel better. Is not this so? And yet it is a mistake. You are sure to be

Painting of Lincoln's cabinet by Francis Carpenter, documenting the first reading of the Emancipation Proclamation. Left to right: Edwin Stanton, secretary of war; Salmon Chase, secretary of the treasury; Lincoln; Gideon Welles, secretary of the navy; Caleb Smith, secretary of the interior; William Seward, secretary of state; Montgomery Blair, postmaster general; Edward Bates, attorney general.

happy again. To know this, which is certainly true, will make you some less miserable now. I have had experience enough to know what I say; and you need only to believe it, to feel better at once. The memory of your dear Father, instead of an agony, will yet be a sad sweet feeling in your heart, of a purer, and holier sort than you have known before.

Please present my kind regards to your afflicted mother.[9]

Emancipation Proclamation (final version), "I invoke the considerate judgment of mankind, and the gracious favor of Almighty God."

January 1, 1863
By the President of the United States of America:
A Proclamation.

Whereas, on the twentysecond day of September, in the year of our Lord one thousand eight hundred and sixty two, a proclamation was issued by the President of the United States, containing, among other things, the following, towit:

"That on the first day of January, in the year of our Lord one thousand eight hundred and sixty-three, all persons held as slaves within any State or designated part of a State, the people whereof shall then be in rebellion against the United States, shall be then, thenceforward, and forever free; and the Executive Government of the United States, including the military and naval authority thereof, will recognize and maintain the freedom of such persons, and will do no act or acts to repress such persons, or any of them, in any efforts they may make for their actual freedom.

"That the Executive will, on the first day of January aforesaid, by proclamation, designate the States and parts of States, if any, in which the people thereof, respectively, shall then be in rebellion against the United States; and the fact that any State, or the people thereof, shall on that day be, in good faith, represented in the Congress of the United States by members chosen thereto at elections wherein a majority of the qualified voters of such State shall have participated, shall, in the absence of strong countervailing testimony, be deemed conclusive evidence that such State, and the people thereof, are not then in rebellion against the United States."

Now, therefore I, Abraham Lincoln, President of the United States, by virtue of the power in me vested as Commander-in-Chief, of the Army and Navy of the United States in time of actual armed rebellion against authority and government of the United States, and as a fit and necessary war measure for suppressing said rebellion, do, on this first day of January, in the year of our Lord one thousand eight hundred and sixty three, and in accordance with my purpose so to do publicly proclaimed for the full period of one hundred days, from the day first above mentioned, order and designate as the States and parts of States wherein the people thereof respectively, are this day in rebellion against the United States, the following, towit:

Arkansas, Texas, Louisiana, (except the Parishes of St. Bernard, Plaquemines, Jefferson, St. Johns, St. Charles, St. James[,] Ascension, Assumption, Terrebonne, Lafourche, St. Mary, St. Martin, and Orleans, including the City of New-Orleans) Mississippi, Alabama, Florida, Georgia, South-Carolina, North-Carolina, and Virginia, (except the fortyeight counties designated as West Virginia, and also the counties of Berkley, Accomac, Northampton, Elizabeth-City, York, Princess Ann, and Norfolk, including the cities of Norfolk & Portsmouth[)]; and which excepted parts are, for the present, left precisely as if this proclamation were not issued.

And by virtue of the power, and for the purpose aforesaid, I do order and declare that all persons held as slaves within said designated States, and parts of States, are, and henceforward shall be free; and that the Executive government of the United States, including the military and naval authorities thereof, will recognize and maintain the freedom of said persons.

And I hereby enjoin upon the people so declared to be free to abstain from all violence, unless in necessary self-defence; and I recommend to them that, in all cases when allowed, they labor faithfully for reasonable wages.

And I further declare and make known, that such persons of suitable condition, will be received into the armed service of the United States to garrison forts, positions, stations, and other places, and to man vessels of all sorts in said service.

And upon this act, sincerely believed to be an act of justice, warranted by the Constitution, upon military necessity, I invoke the considerate judgment of mankind, and the gracious favor of Almighty God.

In witness whereof, I have hereunto set my hand and caused the seal of the United States to be affixed.[10]

Letter to the workingmen of Manchester, England, "an instance of sublime Christian heroism . . ."

January 19, 1863

I have the honor to acknowledge the receipt of the address and resolutions which you sent to me on the eve of the new year.

When I came, on the fourth day of March, 1861, through a free and constitutional election, to preside in the government of the United States, the country was found at the verge of civil war. Whatever might have been the cause, or whosoever the fault, one duty paramount to all others was before me, namely, to maintain and preserve at once the Constitution and the integrity of the federal republic . . .

I have understood well that the duty of self-preservation rests solely with the American people. But I have at the same time been aware that favor or disfavor of foreign nations might have a material influence in enlarging and prolonging the struggle with disloyal men in which the country is engaged. A fair examination of history has seemed to authorize a belief that the past action and influences of the United States were generally regarded as having been beneficient towards mankind. I have therefore reckoned upon the forbearance of nations. Circumstances, to some of which you kindly allude, induced me especially to expect that if justice and good faith should be practiced by the United States, they would encounter no hostile influence on the part of Great Britain. It is now a pleasant duty to acknowledge the demonstration you have given of your desire that a spirit of peace and amity towards this country may prevail in the councils of your Queen, who is respected and esteemed in your own country only more than she is by the kindred nation which has its home on this side of the Atlantic.

I know and deeply deplore the sufferings which the workingmen at Manchester and in all Europe are called to endure in this crisis. It has been often and studiously represented that the attempt to overthrow this government, which was built upon the foundation of human rights, and to substitute for it one which should rest exclusively on the basis of human slavery, was likely to obtain the favor of Europe. Through the actions of our disloyal citizens the workingmen of Europe have been subjected to a severe trial, for the purpose of forcing their sanction to that attempt. Under these circumstances, I cannot but regard your decisive utterance upon the question as an instance of sublime Christian heroism which has not been surpassed in any age or in any country. It is, indeed, an energetic and reinspiring assurance of the inherent power of truth and of the ultimate and universal triumph of justice, humanity, and freedom. I do not doubt that the sentiments you have expressed will be sustained by your great nation, and, on the other hand, I have no hesitation in assuring you that they will excite admiration, esteem, and the most reciprocal feelings of friendship among the American people. I hail this interchange of sentiment, therefore, as an augury that, whatever else may happen, whatever misfortune may befall your country or my own, the peace and friendship which now exist between the two nations will be, as it shall be my desire to make them, perpetual.[11]

Letter to Major General Joseph Hooker, "I am not quite satisfied with you."

Executive Mansion, Washington, January 26, 1863
Major General Hooker:

I have placed you at the head of the Army of the Potomac. Of course I have done this upon what appear to me to be sufficient reasons. And yet I think it best for you to know that there are some things in regard to which, I am not quite satisfied with you. I believe you to be a brave and a skilful soldier, which, of course, I like. I also believe you do not mix politics with your profession, in which you are right. You have confidence in yourself, which is a valuable, if not an indispensable quality. You are ambitious, which, within reasonable bounds, does good rather than harm. But I think that during Gen. Burnside's command of the Army, you have taken counsel of your ambition, and thwarted him as much as you could, in which you did a great wrong to the country, and to a most meritorious and honorable brother officer. I have heard, in such way as to believe it, of your recently saying that both the Army and the Government needed a Dictator. Of course it was not for this, but in spite of it, that I have given you the command. Only those generals who gain successes, can set up dictators. What I now ask of you is military success, and I will risk the dictatorship. The government will support you to the utmost of it's ability, which is neither more nor less than it has done and will do for all commanders. I much fear that the spirit which you have aided to infuse into the Army, of criticising their Commander, and withholding confidence from him, will now turn upon you. I shall assist you as far as I can, to put it down. Neither you, nor Napoleon, if he were alive again, could get any good out of an army, while such a spirit prevails in it.

And now, beware of rashness. Beware of rashness, but with energy, and sleepless vigilance, go forward, and give us victories.[12]

Letter to Andrew Johnson, "The bare sight of fifty thousand armed, and drilled black soldiers on the banks of the Mississippi, would end the rebellion at once."

Andrew Johnson was the former Democratic senator from Tennessee whom Lincoln appointed as military governor of the seceded state in 1862. In 1864, Lincoln chose Johnson to be his running mate on the Republican presidential ticket.

Private
Executive Mansion, Washington, March 26, 1863
My dear Sir:

I am told you have at least thought of raising a negro military force. In my opinion the country now needs no specific thing so much as some man of your ability, and position, to go to this work. When I speak of your position, I mean that of an eminent citizen of a slave-state, and himself a slave-holder. The colored population is the great available and yet unavailed of, force for restoring the Union. The bare sight of fifty thousand armed, and drilled black soldiers on the banks of the Mississippi, would end the rebellion at once. And who doubts that we can present that sight, if we but take hold in earnest? If you have been thinking of it please do not dismiss the thought.[13]

Telegram to Mary Lincoln, "put 'Tad's' pistol away"

Executive Mansion, Washington, June 9, 1863
Mrs. Lincoln
Philadelphia, Pa.

Think you better put "Tad's" pistol away. I had an ugly dream about him.[14]

Lincoln, seated and holding a book, with his son Tad (Thomas) leaning on a table, photographed by Alexander Gardner in February 1865.

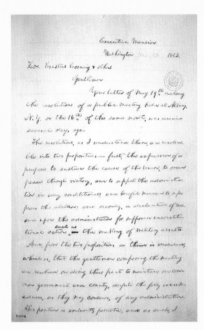

The first page of Lincoln's letter to
Erastus Corning, June 12, 1863.

*Letter responding to resolutions submitted
by Erastus Corning and others, "Must I shoot
a simple-minded soldier boy who deserts,
while I must not touch a hair of a wiley
agitator who induces him to desert?"*

*Erastus Corning, an Albany, New York–based businessman and a Democratic
politician, led a protest meeting against military arrests authorized by Lincoln,
and against the general suspension of habeus corpus.*

Executive Mansion, Washington [June 12,] 1863
Hon. Erastus Corning & others

. . . The resolutions, as I understand them, are resolvable into two propositions—first, the expression of a purpose to sustain the cause of the Union, to
secure peace through victory, and to support the administration in every
constitutional, and lawful measure to suppress the rebellion; and secondly, a

declaration of censure upon the administration for supposed unconstitutional action such as the making of military arrests.

. . . And here I ought to close this paper, and would close it, if there were no apprehension that more injurious consequences, than any merely personal to myself, might follow the censures systematically cast upon me for doing what, in my view of duty, I could not forbear. The resolutions promise to support me in every constitutional and lawful measure to suppress the rebellion; and I have not knowingly employed, nor shall knowingly employ, any other. But the meeting, by their resolutions, assert and argue, that certain military arrests and proceedings following them for which I am ultimately responsible, are unconstitutional. I think they are not.

. . . The arrests were made on totally different grounds, and the proceedings following, accorded with the grounds of the arrests. Let us consider the real case with which we are dealing, and apply to it the parts of the constitution plainly made for such cases.

. . . Prior to my instalation here it had been inculcated that any State had a lawful right to secede from the national Union; and that it would be expedient to exercise the right, whenever the devotees of the doctrine should fail to elect a President to their own liking. I was elected contrary to their liking; and accordingly, so far as it was legally possible, they had taken seven states out of the Union, had seized many of the United States Forts, and had fired upon the United States' Flag, all before I was inaugerated; and, of course, before I had done any official act whatever. The rebellion, thus began soon ran into the present civil war; and, in certain respects, it began on very unequal terms between the parties. The insurgents had been preparing for it more than thirty years, while the government had taken no steps to resist them. The former had carefully considered all the means which could be turned to their account. It undoubtedly was a well pondered reliance with them that in their own unrestricted effort to destroy Union, constitution, and law, all together, the government would, in great degree, be restrained by the same constitution and law, from arresting their progress.

. . . Yet, thoroughly imbued with a reverence for the guarranteed rights of individuals, I was slow to adopt the strong measures, which by degrees I have been forced to regard as being within the exceptions of the constitution, and as indispensable to the public Safety.

. . . Ours is a case of Rebellion—so called by the resolutions before me—in fact, a clear, flagrant, and gigantic case of Rebellion; and the provision of the constitution that "The previlege of the writ of Habeas Corpus shall not be suspended, unless when in cases of Rebellion or Invasion, the public Safety may require it" is the provision which specially applies to our present case. This provision plainly attests the understanding of those who made the constitution that ordinary courts of justice are inadequate to "cases of Rebellion"—attests their purpose that in such cases, men may be held in custody whom the courts acting on ordinary rules, would discharge. Habeas Corpus, does not discharge men who are proved to be guilty of defined crime; and its suspension is allowed by the constitution on purpose that, men may be arrested and held, who can not be proved to be guilty of defined crime, "when, in cases of Rebellion or Invasion the public Safety may require it." This is precisely our present case—a case of Rebellion, wherein the public Safety does require the suspension.

. . . Long experience has shown that armies can not be maintained unless desertion shall be punished by the severe penalty of death. The case requires, and the law and the constitution, sanction this punishment. Must I shoot a simple-minded soldier boy who deserts, while I must not touch a hair of a wiley agitator who induces him to desert?

. . . I can no more be persuaded that the government can constitutionally take no strong measure in time of rebellion, because it can be shown that the same could not be lawfully taken in time of peace, than I can be persuaded that a particular drug is not good medicine for a sick man, because it can be shown to not be good food for a well one. Nor am I able to appreciate the danger, apprehended by the meeting, that the American people will, by means of military arrests during the rebellion, lose the right of public discussion, the liberty of speech and the press, the law of evidence, trial by jury, and Habeas corpus, throughout the indefinite peaceful future which I trust lies before them, any more than I am able to believe that a man could contract so strong an appetite for emetics during temporary illness, as to persist in feeding upon them through the remainder of his healthful life.

. . . In this time of national peril I would have preferred to meet you upon a level one step higher than any party platform; because I am sure that from such more elevated position, we could do better battle for the country we all love, than we possibly can from those lower ones, where from the force of habit, the prejudices of the past, and selfish hopes of the future, we are sure to expend much of our ingenuity and strength, in finding fault with, and aiming blows at each other.[15]

To Ulysses S. Grant, "you were right, and I was wrong."

Executive Mansion, Washington, July 13, 1863
My dear General

I do not remember that you and I ever met personally. I write this now as a grateful acknowledgment for the almost inestimable service you have done the country. I wish to say a word further. When you first reached the vicinity of Vicksburg, I thought you should do, what you finally did—march the troops across the neck, run the batteries with the transports, and thus go below; and I never had any faith, except a general hope that you knew better than I, that the Yazoo Pass expedition, and the like, could succeed. When you got below, and took Port Gibson, Grand Gulf, and vicinity, I thought you should go down the river and join Gen. Banks; and when you turned Northward East of the Big Black, I feared it was a mistake. I now wish to make the personal acknowledgment that you were right, and I was wrong.[16]

Unsent letter to Major General George G. Meade, "He was within your easy grasp . . ."

Executive Mansion, Washington, July 14, 1863
Major General Meade

I have just seen your despatch to Gen. Halleck, asking to be relieved of your command, because of a supposed censure of mine. I am very—very—grateful to you for the magnificent success you gave the cause of the country at Gettysburg; and I am sorry now to be the author of the slightest pain to you. But I was in such deep distress myself that I could not restrain some expression of it. I had been oppressed nearly ever since the battles at Gettysburg, by what appeared to be evidences that yourself, and Gen. Couch, and Gen. Smith [Major General Darius Nash Couch, then commander of the Department of the Susquehanna, and Brigadier General William Farrar "Baldy" Smith], were not seeking a collision with the enemy, but were trying to get him across the river without another battle. What these evidences were, if you please, I hope to tell you at some time, when we shall both feel better. The case, summarily stated is this. You fought and beat the enemy at Gettysburg; and, of course, to say the least, his loss was as great as yours. He retreated; and you did not, as it seemed to me, pressingly pursue him; but a flood in the river detained him, till, by slow degrees, you were again upon him. You had at least twenty thousand veteran troops directly with you, and as many more raw ones within supporting distance, all in addition to those who fought with you at Gettysburg; while it was not possible that he had received a single recruit; and yet you stood and let the flood run down, bridges be built, and the enemy move away at his leisure, without attacking him. And Couch and Smith! The latter left Carlisle in time, upon all ordinary calculation, to have aided you in the last battle at

George Gordon Meade (1815–1872), a career army officer, served both in the Second Seminole War and the Mexican-American War before becoming a brigade commander in the Union army at the outset of the war. Lincoln promoted him to the command of the Army of the Potomac just before the battle of Gettysburg. Meade was trained as an engineer, serving in the Army Corps of Engineers before the outbreak of the Civil War. He designed lighthouses and breakwaters in Florida, including the Jupiter Inlet Lighthouse and the Sombrero Key Lighthouse, and in New Jersey—the Absecon Lighthouse in Atlantic City and the Barnegat Lighthouse on Long Beach Island.

Gettysburg; but he did not arrive. At the end of more than ten days, I believe twelve, under constant urging, he reached Hagerstown from Carlisle, which is not an inch over fiftyfive miles, if so much. And Couch's movement was very little different.

Again, my dear general, I do not believe you appreciate the magnitude of the misfortune involved in Lee's escape. He was within your easy grasp, and to have closed upon him would, in connection with our other late successes, have ended the war. As it is, the war will be prolonged indefinitely. If you could not safely attack Lee last monday, how can you possibly do so South of the river, when you can take with you very few more than two thirds of the force you then had in hand? It would be unreasonable to expect, and I do not expect you can now effect much. Your golden opportunity is gone, and I am distressed immeasureably because of it.

I beg you will not consider this a prossecution, or persecution of yourself. As you had learned that I was dissatisfied, I have thought it best to kindly tell you why.[17]

Verse on Lee's Invasion of the North

July 19, 1863
Gen. Lees invasion of the North written by himself—

In eighteen sixty three, with pomp,
and mighty swell,
Me and Jeff's Confederacy, went
forth to sack Phil-del,
The Yankees they got arter us, and
giv us particular hell,
And we skedaddled back again,
And didn't sack Phil-del.[18]

Elated with the news of the recent defeat of Robert E. Lee's forces at Gettysburg, Pennsylvania, Lincoln dashed off a celebratory ditty in the voice of General Lee.

Gen. Lees invasion of the
North, written by himself—

"In eighteen sixty three, with pomp,
            and mighty swell,
My and Jeff's Confederacy, went
            forth to sack Phil-del,
The Yankees, they got arter us, and
            giv us particuler hell,
And we skedaddled back again,
            and didn't sack Phil-del.

Written Sunday morning July 19. 1863.
        Attest   John Hay.

Order of Retaliation, "a relapse into barbarism and a crime against the civilization of the age."

Executive Mansion, Washington D.C., July 30, 1863

It is the duty of every government to give protection to its citizens, of whatever class, color, or condition, and especially to those who are duly organized as soldiers in the public service. The law of nations and the usages and customs of war as carried on by civilized powers, permit no distinction as to color in the treatment of prisoners of war as public enemies. To sell or enslave any captured person, on account of his color, and for no offence against the laws of war, is a relapse into barbarism and a crime against the civilization of the age.

The government of the United States will give the same protection to all its soldiers, and if the enemy shall sell or enslave anyone because of his color, the offense shall be punished by retaliation upon the enemy's prisoners in our possession.

It is therefore ordered that for every soldier of the United States killed in violation of the laws of war, a rebel soldier shall be executed; and for every one enslaved by the enemy or sold into slavery, a rebel soldier shall be placed at hard labor on the public works and continued at such labor until the other shall be released and receive the treatment due to a prisoner of war[.][19]

To Mary Todd Lincoln, "This is the last we know of poor 'Nanny'"

Executive Mansion, Washington, August 8, 1863

My dear Wife. All as well as usual, and no particular trouble any way. I put the money into the Treasury at five per cent, with the previlege of withdrawing it any time upon thirty days' notice. I suppose you are glad to learn this. Tell dear Tad, poor "Nanny Goat," is lost; and Mrs. Cuthbert & I are in distress about it. The day you left Nanny was found resting herself, and chewing her little cud, on the middle of Tad's bed. But now she's gone! The gardener kept complaining that she destroyed the flowers, till it was concluded to bring her down to the White House. This was done, and the second day she had disappeared, and has not been heard of since. This is the last we know of poor "Nanny[.]"[20]

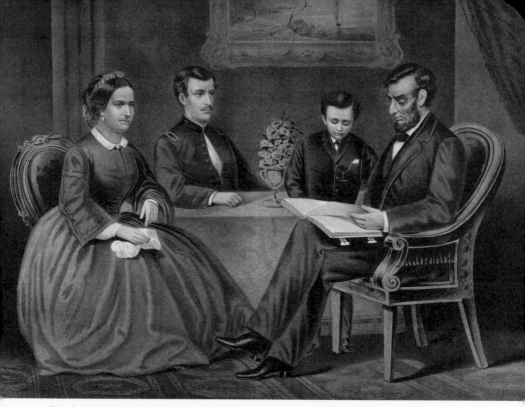

This Currier & Ives print, based on an 1864 photo of the president and his youngest son, Tad, presents an idealized scene of Lincoln reading to his family. The print was published two years after Lincoln's death in 1865.

Letter to James C. Conkling of Springfield, Illinois, "to be plain, you are dissatisfied with me about the negro."

Unable to leave Washington to attend a pro-Union rally organized by Conkling, Lincoln sent this letter with a cover note that read, "You are one of the best public readers. I have but one suggestion. Read it very slowly. And now God bless you, and all good Union-men."

Executive Mansion, Washington, August 26, 1863
My Dear Sir.

. . . There are those who are dissatisfied with me. To such I would say: You desire peace; and you blame me that we do not have it. But how can we attain it? There are but three conceivable ways. First, to suppress the rebellion by force of arms. This, I am trying to do. Are you for it? If you are, so far we are agreed. If you are not for it, a second way is, to give up the Union. I am against this. Are you for it? If you are, you should say so plainly. If you are not for force, nor yet for dissolution, there only remains some imaginable compromise. I do not believe any compromise, embracing the maintenance of the Union, is now possible. All I learn, leads to a directly opposite belief.

. . . But, to be plain, you are dissatisfied with me about the negro. Quite likely there is a difference of opinion between you and myself upon that subject. I certainly wish that all men could be free, while I suppose you do not. Yet I have neither adopted, nor proposed any measure, which is not consistent with even your view, provided you are for the Union. I suggested compensated emancipation; to which you replied you wished not to be taxed to buy negroes. But I had not asked you to be taxed to buy negroes, except in such way, as to save you from greater taxation to save the Union exclusively by other means.

You dislike the emancipation proclamation; and, perhaps, would have it retracted. You say it is unconstitutional—I think differently. I think the constitution invests its commander-in-chief, with the law of war, in time of war. The most that can be said, if so much, is, that slaves are property. Is there—has there ever been—any question that by the law of war, property, both of enemies and friends, may be taken when needed? And is it not needed whenever taking it, helps us, or hurts the enemy? Armies, the world over, destroy enemies' property when they can not use it; and even destroy their own to keep it from the enemy. Civilized belligerents do all in their power to help themselves, or hurt the enemy, except a few things regarded as barbarous or cruel. Among the exceptions are the massacre of vanquished foes, and non-combatants, male and female.

But the proclamation, as law, either is valid, or is not valid. If it is not valid, it needs no retraction. If it is valid, it can not be retracted, any more than the dead can be brought to life. Some of you profess to think its retraction would operate favorably for the Union. Why better after the retraction, than before the issue? There was more than a year and a half of trial to suppress the rebellion before the proclamation issued, the last one hundred days of which passed under an explicit notice that it was coming, unless averted by those in revolt, returning to their allegiance. The war has certainly progressed as favorably for us, since the issue of the proclamation as before. I know as fully as one can know the opinions of others, that some of the commanders of our armies in the field who have given us our most important successes, believe the emancipation policy, and the use of colored troops, constitute the heaviest blow yet dealt to the rebellion; and that, at least one of those important successes, could not have been achieved when it was, but for the aid of black soldiers. Among the commanders holding these views are some who have never had any affinity with what is called abolitionism, or with republican party politics; but who hold them purely as military opinions. I submit these opinions as being entitled to some weight against the objections, often urged, that emancipation, and arming the blacks, are unwise as military measures, and were not adopted, as such, in good faith.

You say you will not fight to free negroes. Some of them seem willing to fight for you; but, no matter. Fight you, then, exclusively to save the Union. I issued the proclamation on purpose to aid you in saving the Union. Whenever you shall have conquered all resistance to the Union, if I shall urge you to continue fighting, it will be an apt time, then, for you to declare you will not fight to free negroes.

I thought that in your struggle for the Union, to whatever extent the negroes should cease helping the enemy, to that extent it weakened the enemy in his resistance to you. Do you think differently? I thought that whatever negroes can be got to do as soldiers, leaves just so much less for white soldiers to do, in saving the Union. Does it appear otherwise to you? But negroes, like other people, act upon motives. Why should they do any thing for us, if we will do nothing for them? If they stake their lives for us, they must be prompted by the strongest motive—even the promise of freedom. And the promise being made, must be kept.

. . . Peace does not appear so distant as it did. I hope it will come soon, and come to stay; and so come as to be worth the keeping in all future time. It will then have been proved that, among free men, there can be no successful appeal from the ballot to the bullet; and that they who take such appeal are sure to lose their case, and pay the cost. And then, there will be some black men who can remember that, with silent tongue, and clenched teeth, and steady eye, and well-poised bayonet, they have helped mankind on to this great consummation; while, I fear, there will be some white ones, unable to forget that, with malignant heart, and deceitful speech, they have strove to hinder it.

Still let us not be over-sanguine of a speedy final triumph. Let us be quite sober. Let us diligently apply the means, never doubting that a just God, in his own good time, will give us the rightful result.[21]

To Salmon P. Chase, "Would I not thus be in the boundless field of absolutism?"

Executive Mansion, Washington, September 2, 1863
My dear Sir:

Knowing your great anxiety that the emancipation proclamation shall now be applied to certain parts of Virginia and Louisiana which were exempted from it last January, I state briefly what appear to me to be difficulties in the way of such a step. The original proclamation has no constitutional or legal justification, except as a military measure. The exemptions were made because the military necessity did not apply to the exempted localities. Nor does that necessity apply to them now any more than it did then. If I take the step must I not do so, without the argument of military necessity, and so, without any argument, except the one that I think the measure politically expedient, and morally right? Would I not thus give up all footing upon constitution or law? Would I not thus be in the boundless field of absolutism? Could this pass unnoticed, or unresisted? Could it fail to be perceived that without any further stretch, I might do the same in Delaware, Maryland, Kentucky, Tennessee, and Missouri; and even change any law in any state? Would not many of our own friends shrink away appalled? Would it not lose us the elections, and with them, the very cause we seek to advance?[22]

Mary Todd Lincoln (1818–1882), here shown in a photograph taken during Lincoln's presidency, was known to be a highly intelligent but emotionally volatile woman. Some modern scholars believe that she suffered from bipolar disorder. Relations between the Lincolns, never warm, were strained by the constant traveling that Lincoln was required to do while a lawyer on the Illinois circuit, and by the death of their son Eddie, in 1850, a month shy of his fourth birthday, and later, by the death of their son Willie, in 1862, at age eleven. Her lavish spending on clothing (as exemplified by the gown in the photo) and on decorating the White House angered Lincoln and undoubtedly cost her in public esteem.

Letter to Mary Lincoln,
"I really wish to see you."

Executive Mansion, Washington, Sep. 22, 1863
Mrs. A. Lincoln.
Fifth Avenue House New-York.

Did you receive my despatch of yesterday? Mrs. Cuthbert did not correctly understand me. I directed her to tell you to use your own pleasure whether to stay or come; and I did not say it is sickly & that you should on no account come. So far as I see or know, it was never healthier, and I really wish to see you. Answer this on receipt.[23]

Letter to James H. Hackett,
"I am used to it."

Lincoln had seen the actor James Hackett portray Falstaff in a production of Henry IV *some months before, and had written Hackett a complimentary letter after Hackett sent him a copy of a book that he had authored. Hackett publicized Lincoln's letter, and Lincoln was widely ridiculed for his supposed philistinism. In fact, he was a keen student of Shakespeare's works, and had committed several soliloquies to memory.*

Private
Executive Mansion, Washington, Nov. 2, 1863.
My dear Sir:

. . . Give yourself no uneasiness on the subject mentioned in [your letter] of the 22nd.

My note to you I certainly did not expect to see in print; yet I have not been much shocked by the newspaper comments upon it. Those comments constitute a fair specimen of what has occurred to me through life. I have endured a great deal of ridicule without much malice; and have received a great deal of kindness, not quite free from ridicule. I am used to it.[24]

The actor James Hackett
as Falstaff, c. 1859.

*Address delivered at the dedication
of the cemetery at Gettysburg—
Three Versions*

Executive Mansion,

Washington,   , 186 .

Four score and seven years ago our fathers brought
forth, upon this continent, a new nation, conceived
in liberty, and dedicated to the proposition that
"all men are created equal"

Now we are engaged in a great civil war, testing
whether that nation, or any nation so conceived,
and so dedicated, can long endure. We are met
on a great battle field of that war. We have
come to dedicate a portion of it, as a final resting place for those who died here, that the nation
might live. This we may, in all propriety do. But, in a
larger sense, we can not dedicate— we can not
consecrate— we can not hallow, this ground—
The brave men, living and dead, who struggled
here, have hallowed it, far above our poor power
to add or detract. The world will little note, nor long
remember what we say here; while it can never
forget what they did here.
It is rather for us, the living, to stand here,

There are five known handwritten copies of Lincoln's oration at Gettysburg, each of these "autograph" copies differing slightly from the other. Lincoln gave one copy to each of his secretaries, John Nicolay and John Hay. The first of these, the "Nicolay Copy," (previous page) was written prior to the day that Lincoln delivered the address. The first sheet is on Executive Mansion letterhead, the second on foolscap, most likely reworked from the original. The second (the "Hay Copy" this page) is thought by scholars to have been written by Lincoln just after the event. It more closely resembles other contemporaneous accounts of the speech than the Nicolay version. The other three were written by Lincoln well after the fact for the purposes of charitable fundraising. The "Bliss Copy," (next page) named, like the others, for the person to whom Lincoln gave the manuscript, is considered by most historians to be the "final" draft because of the care with which Lincoln prepared it, coupled with the fact that he titled, signed, and dated it. The historian Garry Wills notes that Lincoln was forever revising and improving his written texts and speeches, and that this draft can be considered to be the one that best represents Lincoln's intended message. This is the text that is inscribed on the base of the Lincoln Memorial on the National Mall in Washington, D.C.

The Nicolay and Hay manuscripts are in the collection of the Library of Congress; the "Everett Copy," given by Lincoln to the featured speaker at Gettysburg, Edward Everett, is in the collection of the Abraham Lincoln Presidential Library and Museum in Springfield, Illinois. Lincoln created the "Bancroft Copy" for the historian George Bancroft, but it could not be used for reproduction because Lincoln wrote on both sides of the paper. Bancroft was allowed to keep the document, which has since been donated to the Carl A. Kroch Library at Cornell University. Lincoln rewrote the text a final time, now on separate sheets. He gave this copy to Bancroft's stepson, Alexander Bliss, for publication. The "Bliss Copy" is on display in the Lincoln Room of the White House.

Four score and seven years ago our fathers brought forth, on this continent, a new nation, conceived in Liberty, and dedicated to the proposition that all men are created equal.

Now we are engaged in a great civil war, testing whether that nation, or any nation so conceived, and so dedicated, can long endure. We are met on a great battle-field of that war. We have come to dedicate a portion of that field, as a final resting-place for those who here gave their lives, that that nation might live. It is altogether fitting and proper that we should do this.

But, in a larger sense, we can not dedicate — we can not consecrate — we can not hallow — this ground. The brave men, living and dead, who struggled here, have consecrated it far above our poor power to add or detract. The world will little note, nor long remember what we say here, but it can never forget what they did here. It is for us the living, rather, to be dedicated here to the unfinished work which they who fought here have thus far so nobly advanced. It is rather for us to be here dedicated to the great task remaining be-

FIRST DRAFT
Executive Mansion, Washington, 1863

Four score and seven years ago our fathers brought forth, upon this continent, a new nation, conceived in liberty, and dedicated to the proposition that "all men are created equal."

Now we are engaged in a great civil war, testing whether that nation, or any nation so conceived, and so dedicated, can long endure. We are met on a great battle field of that war. We have come to dedicate a portion of it, as a final resting place for those who died here, that the nation might live. This we may, in all propriety do. But, in a larger sense, we can not dedicate—we can not consecrate—we can not hallow, this ground. The brave men, living and dead, who struggled here, have hallowed it, far above our poor power to add or detract. The world will little note, nor long remember what we say here; while it can never forget what they did here.

It is rather for us, the living, we here be dedicated to the great task remaining before us—that, from these honored dead we take increased devotion to that cause for which they here, gave the last full measure of devotion—that we here highly resolve these dead shall not have died in vain; that the nation, shall have a new birth of freedom, and that government of the people by the people for the people, shall not perish from the earth.

FINAL TEXT
Address delivered at the dedication of the cemetery at Gettysburg.

Four score and seven years ago our fathers brought forth on this continent, a new nation, conceived in Liberty, and dedicated to the proposition that all men are created equal.

Now we are engaged in a great civil war, testing whether that nation, or any nation so conceived and so dedicated, can long endure. We are met on a great battle-field of that war. We have come to dedicate a portion of that field, as a final resting place for those who here gave their lives that that nation might live. It is altogether fitting and proper that we should do this.

But, in a larger sense, we can not dedicate—we can not consecrate—we can not hallow—this ground. The brave men, living and dead, who struggled here, have consecrated it, far above our poor power to add or detract. The world will little note, nor long remember what we say here, but it can never forget what they did here. It is for us the living, rather, to be dedicated here to the unfinished work which they who fought here have thus far so nobly advanced. It is rather for us to be here dedicated to the great task remaining before us—that from these honored dead we take increased devotion to that cause for which they gave the last full measure of devotion—that we here highly resolve that these dead shall not have died in vain—that this nation, under God, shall have a new birth of freedom—and that government of the people, by the people, for the people, shall not perish from the earth.[25]

A bareheaded Lincoln among the crowd at Gettysburg, seated to the left of the bearded, tophatted gentleman standing near the center of the photograph.

To Edward Everett, "I am pleased to know that . . . the little I did say was not entirely a failure."

Everett, a former governor of Massachusetts, U.S. secretary of state and senator, and president of Harvard University, was the featured speaker at Gettysburg. In a letter to Lincoln, he had written that "I should be glad, if I could flatter myself that I came as near to the central idea of the occasion, in two hours, as you did in two minutes."

Executive Mansion, Washington, Nov. 20, 1863
My dear Sir:

Your kind note of to-day is received. In our respective parts yesterday, you could not have been excused to make a short address, nor I a long one. I am pleased to know that, in your judgment, the little I did say was not entirely a failure. Of course I knew Mr. Everett would not fail; and yet, while the whole discourse was eminently satisfactory, and will be of great value, there were passages in it which trancended my expectation. The point made against the theory of the general government being only an agency, whose principals are the States, was new to me, and, as I think, is one of the best arguments for the national supremacy. The tribute to our noble women for their angel-ministering to the suffering soldiers, surpasses, in its way, as do the subjects of it, whatever has gone before.

Our sick boy, for whom you kindly inquire, we hope is past the worst.[26]

To Salmon P. Chase, "I have known just as little of these things as my own friends have allowed me to know."

Lincoln responds to evidence that Chase, his treasury secretary, had been involved in an attempt to replace Lincoln as the Republican presidential candidate in 1864—"Mr. Pomeroy's letter."

Executive Mansion, Washington, February 29, 1864
My dear Sir:

I would have taken time to answer yours of the 22nd. sooner, only that I did not suppose any evil could result from the delay, especially as, by a note, I promptly acknowled[ged] the receipt of yours, and promised a fuller answer. Now, on consideration, I find there is really very little to say. My knowledge of Mr. Pomeroy's letter having been made public came to me only the day you wrote; but I had, in spite of myself, known of it's existence several days before. I have not yet read it, and I think I shall not. I was not shocked, or surprised by the appearance of the letter, because I had had knowledge of Mr. Pomeroy's Committee, and of secret issues which I supposed came from it, and of secret agents who I supposed were sent out by it, for several weeks. I have known just as little of these things as my own friends have allowed me to know. They bring the documents to me, but I do not read them—they tell me what they think fit to tell me, but I do not inquire for more. I fully concur with you that neither of us can be justly held responsible for what our respective friends may do without our instigation or countenance; and I assure you, as you have assured me, that no assault has been made upon you by my instigation, or with my countenance.

Whether you shall remain at the head of the Treasury Department is a question which I will not allow myself to consider from any stand-point other than my judgment of the public service; and, in that view, I do not perceive occasion for a change.[27]

To Michael Hahn, "I barely suggest for your private consideration . . ."

Lincoln urges Michael Hahn, the newly elected governor of "free-state" Louisiana, to consider giving blacks the right to vote. Louisiana was the first of the seceded states to rejoin the Union.

Private
Executive Mansion, Washington, March 13, 1864
My dear Sir:

I congratulate you on having fixed your name in history as the first-free-state Governor of Louisiana. Now you are about to have a Convention which, among other things, will probably define the elective franchise. I barely suggest for your private consideration, whether some of the colored people may not be let in—as, for instance, the very intelligent, and especially those who have fought gallantly in our ranks. They would probably help, in some trying time to come, to keep the jewel of liberty within the family of freedom. But this is only a suggestion, not to the public, but to you alone.[28]

To Albert G. Hodges, "I claim not to have controlled events, but confess plainly that events have controlled me."

Executive Mansion, Washington, April 4, 1864
A. G. Hodges, Esq.
Frankfort, Ky.

My dear Sir: You ask me to put in writing the substance of what I verbally said the other day, in your presence, to Governor Bramlette and Senator Dixon. It was about as follows:

"I am naturally anti-slavery. If slavery is not wrong, nothing is wrong. I can not remember when I did not so think, and feel. And yet I have never understood that the Presidency conferred upon me an unrestricted right to act officially upon this judgment and feeling. It was in the oath I took that I would, to the best of my ability, preserve, protect, and defend the Constitution of the United States. I could not take the office without taking the oath. Nor was it my view that I might take an oath to get power, and break the oath in using the power. I understood, too, that in ordinary civil administration this oath even forbade me to practically indulge my primary abstract judgment on the moral question of slavery. I had publicly declared this many times, and in many ways. And I aver that, to this day, I have done no official act in mere deference to my abstract judgment and feeling on slavery. I did understand however, that my oath to preserve the constitution to the best of my ability, imposed upon me the duty of preserving, by every indispensable means, that government—that nation—of which that constitution was the organic law. Was it possible to lose the nation, and yet preserve the constitution? By general law life and limb must be protected; yet often a limb must be amputated to save a life; but a life is never wisely given to save a limb. I felt that measures, otherwise unconstitutional, might become lawful, by becoming indispensable to the preservation of the constitution, through the preservation of the nation. Right or wrong, I assumed this ground, and now avow it. I could not feel that, to the best of my ability, I had even tried to preserve the constitution, if, to save slavery, or any minor matter, I should permit the wreck of government, country, and Constitution all together. When, early in the war, Gen. Frémont attempted military emancipation, I forbade it, because I did not then think it an indispensable necessity. When a little later, Gen. Cameron, then Secretary of War, suggested the arming of the blacks, I objected, because I did not yet think it an indispensable necessity. When, still later, Gen. Hunter attempted military emancipation, I again forbade it, because I did not yet think the indispensable necessity had come. When, in March, and May, and July 1862 I made earnest, and successive appeals to the border states to favor compensated emancipation, I believed the indispensable necessity for military emancipation, and arming the blacks would come, unless averted by that measure. They declined the proposition; and I was, in my best judgment, driven to the alternative of either surrendering the Union, and with it, the Constitution, or of laying strong hand upon the colored element. I chose the latter. In choosing it, I hoped for greater gain than loss; but of this, I was not entirely confident. More than a year of trial now shows no loss by it in our foreign relations, none in our home popular sentiment, none in our white military force,—no loss by it any how or any where. On the contrary, it shows a gain of quite a hundred and thirty thousand soldiers, seamen, and laborers. These are palpable facts, about which, as facts, there can be no cavilling. We have the men; and we could not have had them without the measure.

["]And now let any Union man who complains of the measure, test himself by writing down in one line that he is for subduing the rebellion by force of arms; and in the next, that he is for taking these hundred and thirty thousand men from the Union side, and placing them where they would be but for the measure he condemns. If he can not face his case so stated, it is only because he can not face the truth.["]

I add a word which was not in the verbal conversation. In telling this tale I attempt no compliment to my own sagacity. I claim not to have controlled events, but confess plainly that events have controlled me. Now, at the end of three years struggle the nation's condition is not what either party, or any man devised, or expected. God alone can claim it. Whither it is tending seems plain. If God now wills the removal of a great wrong, and wills also that we of the North as well as you of the South, shall pay fairly for our complicity in that wrong, impartial history will find therein new cause to attest and revere the justice and goodness of God.[29]

To Mrs. Horace Mann,
"He wills to do it."

Mary Tyler Peabody Mann, a writer and advocate for free public kindergartens, was the widow of Horace Mann, the well-known education reformer and the founder of Antioch College.

Washington, April 5, 1864
Madam,

The petition of persons under eighteen, praying that I would free all slave children, and the heading of which petition it appears you wrote, was handed me a few days since by Senator Sumner. Please tell these little people I am very glad their young hearts are so full of just and generous sympathy, and that, while I have not the power to grant all they ask, I trust they will remember that God has, and that, as it seems, He wills to do it.[30]

Address at sanitary fair,
Baltimore, Maryland

April 18, 1864

Ladies and Gentlemen—Calling to mind that we are in Baltimore, we can not fail to note that the world moves. Looking upon these many people, assembled here, to serve, as they best may, the soldiers of the Union, it occurs at once that three years ago, the same soldiers could not so much as pass through Baltimore. The change from then till now, is both great, and gratifying. Blessings on the brave men who have wrought the change, and the fair women who strive to reward them for it.

. . . The world has never had a good definition of the word liberty, and the American people, just now, are much in want of one. We all declare for liberty; but in using the same word we do not all mean the same thing. With some the word liberty may mean for each man to do as he pleases with himself, and the product of his labor; while with others the same word may mean for some men to do as they please with other men, and the product of other men's labor. Here are two, not only different, but incompatable things, called by the same name—

liberty. And it follows that each of the things is, by the respective parties, called by two different and incompatable names—liberty and tyranny.

The shepherd drives the wolf from the sheep's throat, for which the sheep thanks the shepherd as a liberator, while the wolf denounces him for the same act as the destroyer of liberty, especially as the sheep was a black one. Plainly the sheep and the wolf are not agreed upon a definition of the word liberty; and precisely the same difference prevails to-day among us human creatures, even in the North, and all professing to love liberty. Hence we behold the processes by which thousands are daily passing from under the yoke of bondage, hailed by some as the advance of liberty, and bewailed by others as the destruction of all liberty. Recently, as it seems, the people of Maryland have been doing something to define liberty; and thanks to them that, in what they have done, the wolf's dictionary, has been repudiated.[31]

To Ulysses S. Grant, "I begin to see it."

Washington, June 15, 1864
United States Military Telegraph,
Lieut. Gen. Grant War Department.
Head Qrs. A.P.

Have just read your despatch of 1 P.M. yesterday. I begin to see it. You will succeed. God bless you all.[32]

To Mary Todd Lincoln, "Tad and I have been to Gen. Grant's army."

Executive Mansion, Washington, June 24, 1864
Mrs. A. Lincoln
Boston, Mass.

All well, and very warm. Tad and I have been to Gen. Grant's army. Returned yesterday safe and sound.[33]

Memorandum read to cabinet, "and much worse, a wrong to the country."

Lincoln chastises his cabinet for bickering and scheming.

Executive Mansion, Washington, [July 14?], 186[4]

I must myself be the judge, how long to retain in, and when to remove any of you from, his position. It would greatly pain me to discover any of you endeavoring to procure anothers removal, or, in any way to prejudice him before the public. Such endeavor would be a wrong to me; and much worse, a wrong to the country. My wish is that on this subject, no remark be made, nor question asked, by any of you, here or elsewhere, now or hereafter.[34]

To Ulysses S. Grant, "Hold on with a bull-dog gripe [sic] . . ."

"Cypher"
Executive Mansion, Washington, August 17, 1864
Lieut. Gen. Grant
City Point, Va.

I have seen your despatch expressing your unwillingness to break your hold where you are. Neither am I willing. Hold on with a bull-dog gripe [sic], and chew & choke, as much as possible.[35]

Speech to the One Hundred Sixty-Fourth Ohio Regiment, "There is more involved in this contest than is realized by every one."

August 18, 1864

Soldiers—You are about to return to your homes and your friends, after having, as I learn, performed in camp a comparatively short term of duty in this great contest. . . .We have, as all will agree, a free Government, where every man has a right to be equal with every other man. In this great struggle, this form of Government and every form of human right is endangered if our enemies succeed. There is more involved in this contest than is realized by every one. There is involved in this struggle the question whether your children and my children shall enjoy the privileges we have enjoyed. I say this in order to impress upon you, if you are not already so impressed, that no small matter should divert us from our great purpose. There may be some irregularities in the practical application of our system. It is fair that each man shall pay taxes in exact proportion to the value of his property; but if we should wait before collecting a tax to adjust the taxes upon each man in exact proportion with every other man, we should never collect any tax at all. There may be mistakes made sometimes; things may be done wrong while the officers of the Government do all they can to prevent mistakes. But I beg of you, as citizens of this great Republic, not to let your minds be carried off from the great work we have before us. This struggle is too large for you to be diverted from it by any small matter. When you return to your homes rise up to the height of a generation of men worthy of a free Government, and we will carry out the great work we have commenced. I return to you my sincere thanks, soldiers, for the honor you have done me this afternoon.[36]

Memorandum concerning his probable failure of reelection

Executive Mansion,
Washington, Aug. 23, 1864

This morning, as for some days past, it seems exceedingly probable that this Administration will not be re-elected. Then it will be my duty to so co-operate with the President elect, as to save the Union between the election and the inauguration; as he will have secured his election on such ground that he can not possibly save it afterwards.[37]

Executive Mansion,

Washington, Aug. 23, 1864.

This morning, as for some days
past, it seems exceedingly probably that this Administration will
not be re-elected. Then it will
be my duty to so coöperate with
the ~~Government~~. President elect,
as to save the Union between the
election and the inauguration; as
he will have secured his election
on such ground that he cannot
possibly save it afterwards.

A. Lincoln.

To Eliza P. Gurney, "God knows best, and has ruled otherwise."

Executive Mansion, Washington, September 4, 1864
My esteemed friend.

I have not forgotten—probably never shall forget—the very impressive occasion when yourself and friends visited me on a Sabbath forenoon two years ago. Nor has your kind letter, written nearly a year later, ever been forgotten. In all, it has been your purpose to strengthen my reliance on God. I am much indebted to the good christian people of the country for their constant prayers and consolations; and to no one of them, more than to yourself. The purposes of the Almighty are perfect, and must prevail, though we erring mortals may fail to accurately perceive them in advance. We hoped for a happy termination of this terrible war long before this; but God knows best, and has ruled otherwise. We shall yet acknowledge His wisdom and our own error therein. Meanwhile we must work earnestly in the best light He gives us, trusting that so working still conduces to the great ends He ordains. Surely He intends some great good to follow this mighty convulsion, which no mortal could make, and no mortal could stay.

Your people—the Friends—have had, and are having, a very great trial. On principle, and faith, opposed to both war and oppression, they can only practically oppose oppression by war. In this hard dilemma, some have chosen one horn and some the other. For those appealing to me on conscientious grounds, I have done, and shall do, the best I could and can, in my own conscience, under my oath to the law. That you believe this I doubt not; and believing it, I shall still receive, for our country and myself, your earnest prayers to our Father in Heaven.[38]

Copy of Lincoln's memo dated August 23, 1864, on the likelihood of his defeat in the 1864 presidential election. Lincoln mordantly asserts that he must hold the Union together until his opponent takes office because "he will have secured the election on such ground that he cannot possibly save it afterwards."

A commemorative steel engraving and lithograph shows a reproduction or imagined handwritten text of the condolence letter that Lincoln wrote to a Massachussetts woman who lost five sons in the war. The original has never been found, and some scholars have attributed the text to Lincoln's aide, John M. Hay.

Executive Mansion
Washington, Nov 21, 1864

To Mrs Bixby, Boston, Mass,
Dear Madam,
I have been shown in the files of the War Department a statement of the Adjutant General of Massachusetts that you are the mother of five sons who have died gloriously on the field of battle. I feel how weak and fruitless must be any word of mine which should attempt to beguile you from the grief of a loss so overwhelming. But I cannot refrain from tendering you the consolation that may be found in the thanks of the republic they died to save. I pray that our Heavenly Father may assuage the anguish of your bereavement, and leave you only the cherished memory of the loved and lost, and the solemn pride that must be yours to have laid so costly a sacrifice upon the altar of freedom.
Yours very sincerely and respectfully,
A. Lincoln.

To Mrs. Lydia Bixby, "I feel how weak and fruitless must be any words of mine . . ."

Lincoln's condolence letter to a Massachusetts woman whose five sons were supposedly killed in battle; in fact, Lincoln had been misinformed about the Bixby clan's sacrifices.

Executive Mansion,
Washington, Nov. 21, 1864

Dear Madam,—I have been shown in the files of the War Department a statement of the Adjutant General of Massachusetts, that you are the mother of five sons who have died gloriously on the field of battle.

I feel how weak and fruitless must be any words of mine which should attempt to beguile you from the grief of a loss so overwhelming. But I cannot refrain from tendering to you the consolation that may be found in the thanks of the Republic they died to save.

I pray that our Heavenly Father may assuage the anguish of your bereavement, and leave you only the cherished memory of the loved and lost, and the solemn pride that must be yours, to have laid so costly a sacrifice upon the altar of Freedom.[39]

Reply to a delegation of Kentuckians, "Somebody has been howling ever since . . ."

Lincoln replies to a group requesting to be put under the authority of General Benjamin Butler.

January 2, 1865

You howled when Butler went to New-Orleans. Others howled when he was removed from that command. Somebody has been howling ever since at his assignment to military command. How long will it be before you, who are howling for his assignment to rule Kentucky, will be howling to me to remove him?[40]

To Ulysses S. Grant, "answer this letter as though I was not President, but only a friend."

Lincoln asks Grant to find a position in the army for his son Robert.

Executive Mansion, Washington, Jan. 19, 1865
Lieut. General Grant:

Please read and answer this letter as though I was not President, but only a friend. My son, now in his twenty second year, having graduated at Harvard, wishes to see something of the war before it ends. I do not wish to put him in the ranks, nor yet to give him a commission, to which those who have already served long, are better entitled, and better qualified to hold. Could he, without embarrassment to you, or detriment to the service, go into your Military family with some nominal rank, I, and not the public, furnishing his necessary means? If no, say so without the least hesitation, because I am as anxious, and as deeply interested, that you shall not be encumbered as you can be yourself.[41]

To Edwin M. Stanton, "About Jews."

Lincoln smoothes the way for his Jewish chiropodist to be reunited with his family, and urges a hearing for a Jewish officer who had been dismissed from the service with cause in January 1865.

Executive Mansion, Washington Jan. 25, 1865
Hon. Secretary of War.
My dear Sir.

About Jews. I wish you would give Dr. Zacharie a pass to go to Savannah, remain a week and return, bringing with him, if he wishes, his father and sisters or any

Lincoln's son Robert Todd Lincoln, in his military uniform, photographed by Mathew Brady in 1853. Against Mary's wishes, Lincoln arranged for Robert to be given a military commission in the Union army in 1865.

Lincoln's secretary of war, Edward M. Stanton (1814–1869), was a highly successful and ambitious lawyer from Ohio, whom Lincoln sought for his cabinet because he was an antislavery, pro-Union Democrat. Known for his imperious manner and tendency to overmanage, Stanton is widely credited with organizing Union resources into a powerful war machine. Though he and Lincoln were temperamentally opposites, the two men nonetheless enjoyed a good working relationship. Stanton shared with Lincoln a personal history marred by tragedy: his one-and-a-half-year-old daughter died suddenly in 1841, and his wife died suddenly three years later. Stanton remarried a woman fifteen years his junior in 1856. In 1869, President Ulysses S. Grant nominated Stanton to be an associate justice of the United States Supreme Court; Stanton died only days after his confirmation by the Senate, aged fifty-five.

of them. This will spare me trouble and oblige me. I promised him long ago that he should be allowed this whenever Savannah should fall into our hands.

Blumenberg, at Baltimore. I think he should have a hearing. He has suffered for us & served us well—had the rope around his neck for being our friend—raised troops—fought, and been wounded. He should not be dismissed in a way that disgraces and ruins him without a hearing.[42]

To Lieutenant Colonel John Glenn,
"You must not force negroes any more than white men."

"Cypher"
Executive Mansion, Washington, Feb. 7, 1865
Lt. Col. Glenn.
Commanding Post at Henderson, Ky.

Complaint is made to me that you are forcing negroes into the Military service, and even torturing them—riding them on rails and the like—to extort their consent. I hope this may be a mistake. The like must not be done by you, or any one under you. You must not force negroes any more than white men. Answer me on this.[43]

The cover illustration of the March 14, 1863, issue of *Harper's Weekly* shows a black soldier being trained to use a weapon, surely a shocking image for the time.

The crowd at Lincoln's second inaugural, held in front of the east portico of the Capitol building on March 4, 1865. Lincoln stands behind a small lectern on a white pedestal near the center of the photograph, his future assassin John Wilkes Booth is visible behind the front railing of the portico above.

Second Inaugural Address

March 4, 1865
[Fellow Countrymen:]

At this second appearing to take the oath of the presidential office, there is less occasion for an extended address than there was at the first. Then a statement, somewhat in detail, of a course to be pursued, seemed fitting and proper. Now, at the expiration of four years, during which public declarations have been constantly called forth on every point and phase of the great contest which still absorbs the attention, and engrosses the enerergies [sic] of the nation, little that is new could be presented. The progress of our arms, upon which all else chiefly depends, is as well known to the public as to myself; and it is, I trust, reasonably satisfactory and encouraging to all. With high hope for the future, no prediction in regard to it is ventured.

On the occasion corresponding to this four years ago, all thoughts were anxiously directed to an impending civil-war. All dreaded it—all sought to avert it. While the inaugeral address was being delivered from this place, devoted altogether to saving the Union without war, insurgent agents were in the city seeking to destroy it without war—seeking to dissol[v]e the Union, and divide effects, by negotiation. Both parties deprecated war; but one of them would make war rather than let the nation survive; and the other would accept war rather than let it perish. And the war came.

One eighth of the whole population were colored slaves, not distributed generally over the Union, but localized in the Southern part of it. These slaves constituted a peculiar and powerful interest. All knew that this interest was, somehow, the cause of the war. To strengthen, perpetuate, and extend this interest was the object for which the insurgents would rend the Union, even by war; while the government claimed no right to do more than to restrict the territorial enlargement of it. Neither party expected for the war, the magnitude, or the duration, which it has already attained. Neither anticipated that the cause of the conflict might cease with, or even before, the conflict itself should cease. Each looked for an easier triumph, and a result less fundamental and astounding. Both read the same Bible, and pray to the same God; and each invokes His aid against the other. It may seem strange that any men should dare to ask a just God's assistance in wringing their bread from the sweat of other men's faces; but let us judge not that we be not judged. The prayers of both could not be answered; that of neither has been answered fully. The Almighty has His own purposes. "Woe unto the world because of offences! for it must needs be that offences come; but woe to that man by whom the offence cometh!" If we shall suppose that American Slavery is one of those offences which, in the providence of God, must needs come, but which, having continued through His appointed time, He now wills to remove, and that He gives to both North and South, this terrible war, as the woe due to those by whom the offence came, shall we discern therein any departure from those divine attributes which the believers in a Living God always ascribe to Him? Fondly do we hope—fervently do we pray—that this mighty scourge of war may speedily pass away. Yet, if God wills that it continue, until all the wealth piled by the bond-man's two hundred and fifty years of unrequited toil shall be sunk, and until every drop of blood drawn with the lash, shall be paid by another drawn with the sword, as was said three thousand years ago, so still it must be said "the judgments of the Lord, are true and righteous altogether."

With malice toward none; with charity for all; with firmness in the right, as God gives us to see the right, let us strive on to finish the work we are in; to bind up the nation's wounds; to care for him who shall have borne the battle, and for his widow, and his orphan—to do all which may achieve and cherish a just, and a lasting peace, among ourselves, and with all nations.[44]

To Thurlow Weed, "To deny it . . . is to deny that there is a God governing the world."

Weed, the publisher of the Albany Evening Journal, *was a leading Republican (and former Whig) politician from New York.*

Executive Mansion, Washington, March 15, 1865
My dear Sir.

Every one likes a compliment. Thank you for yours on my little notification speech, and on the recent Inaugeral Address. I expect the latter to wear as well as—perhaps better than—any thing I have produced; but I believe it is not immediately popular. Men are not flattered by being shown that there has been a difference of purpose between the Almighty and them. To deny it, however, in this case, is to deny that there is a God governing the world. It is a truth which I thought needed to be told; and as whatever of humiliation there is in it, falls most directly on myself, I thought others might afford for me to tell it.[45]

Speech to the One Hundred Fortieth Indiana Regiment, "I am in favor of giving an opportunity to such white men to try [slavery] on for themselves."

The 140th Indiana Regiment, in Washington following the siege of Murfreesboro, heard Lincoln ruminate on the recently adopted Confederate policy of bringing black soldiers into their army.

March 17, 1865
[Newspaper Version]

FELLOW CITIZENS—It will be but a very few words that I shall undertake to say. I was born in Kentucky, raised in Indiana and lived in Illinois. (Laughter.) And now I am here, where it is my business to care equally for the good people of all the States. I am glad to see an Indiana regiment on this day able to present the captured flag to the Governor of Indiana. (Applause.) I am not disposed, in saying this, to make a distinction between the States, for all have done equally well. (Applause.) There are but few views or aspects of this great war upon which I have not said or written something whereby my own opinions might be known. But there is one—the recent attempt of our erring brethren, as they are sometimes called—(laughter)—to employ the negro to fight for them. I have neither written nor made a speech on that subject, because that was their business, not mine; and if I had a wish upon the subject I had not the power to introduce it, or make it effective. The great question with them was, whether the negro, being put into the army, would fight for them. I do not know, and therefore cannot decide. (Laughter.) They ought to know better than we. I have in my lifetime heard many arguments why the negroes ought to be slaves; but if they fight for those who would keep them in slavery it will be a better argument than any I have yet heard.

(Laughter and applause.) He who will fight for that ought to be a slave. (Applause.) They have concluded at last to take one out of four of the slaves, and put them in the army; and that one out of the four who will fight to keep the others in slavery ought to be a slave himself unless he is killed in a fight. (Applause.) While I have often said that all men ought to be free, yet I would allow those colored persons to be slaves who want to be; and next to them those white persons who argue in favor of making other people slaves. (Applause.) I am in favor of giving an opportunity to such white men to try it on for themselves. (Applause.) I will say one thing in regard to the negro being employed to fight for them. I do know he cannot fight and stay at home and make bread too—(laughter and applause)—and as one is about as important as the other to them, I don't care which they do. (Renewed applause.) I am rather in favor of having them try them as soldiers. (Applause.) They lack one vote of doing that, and I wish I could send my vote over the river so that I might cast it in favor of allowing the negro to fight. (Applause.) But they cannot fight and work both. We must now see the bottom of the enemy's resources. They will stand out as long as they can, and if the negro will fight for them, they must allow him to fight. They have drawn upon their last branch of resources. (Applause.) And we can now see the bottom. (Applause.) I am glad to see the end so near at hand. (Applause.) I have said now more than I intended, and will therefore bid you goodby.[46]

To Mary Todd Lincoln, *"All now looks highly favorable."*

Head Quarters Armies of the United States,
Washington, D.C., April 2, 7/45 [A.M.], 1865,
Mrs. A. Lincoln, City-Point

Last night Gen. Grant telegraphed that Sheridan with his Cavalry and the 5th. Corps had captured three brigades of Infantry, a train of wagons, and several batteries, prisoners amounting to several thousands. This morning Gen. Grant, having ordered an attack along the whole line telegraphs as follows

"Both Wright and Parke got through the enemies lines. The battle now rages furiously. Sheridan with his Cavalry, the 5th. Corps, & Miles Division of the 2nd. Corps, which was sent to him since 1. this A.M. is now sweeping down from the West. All now looks highly favorable. Ord is engaged, but I have not yet heard the result in his front"

Robert yesterday wrote a little cheerful note to Capt. Penrose, which is all I have heard of him since you left.[47]

To Edwin M. Stanton,
"It is certain now that Richmond
is in our hands . . ."

Head Quarters Armies of the United States,
Washington, D.C., April 3, 5 P.M., 1865,
Hon. Sec. of War City-Point

Yours received. Thanks for your caution; but I have already been to Petersburg, staid with Gen. Grant an hour & a half and returned here. It is certain now that Richmond is in our hands, and I think I will go there to-morrow. I will take care of myself.[48]

To John A. Campbell,
"No cessation of hostilities short
of an end of the war . . ."

A native of Georgia by way of Alabama, Campbell was U.S. Supreme Court justice between 1853 and 1861, ruling with the majority in the Dred Scott decision. At the outset of the war, Campbell tried and failed to mediate between the federal government and the seceded states, joining the Confederate States of America as assistant secretary of war in May 1861.

[April 5, 1865]

As to peace, I have said before, and now repeat, that three things are indispensable.

1. The restoration of the national authority throughout all the States.

2. No receding by the Executive of the United States on the slavery question, from the position assumed thereon, in the late Annual Message to Congress, and in preceding documents.

3. No cessation of hostilities short of an end of the war, and the disbanding of all force hostile to the government.

That all propositions coming from those now in hostility to the government; and not inconsistent with the foregoing, will be respectfully considered, and passed upon in a spirit of sincere liberality. . .[49]

Telegram to Ulysses S. Grant, "Let the thing be pressed."

Head Quarters Armies of the United States,
City-Point, April 7, 11 A.M., 1865,
Lieut Gen. Grant.

Gen. Sheridan says "If the thing is pressed I think that Lee will surrender." Let the thing be pressed.[50]

To Gideon Welles

The secretary of the navy is instructed to give the president's son a souvenir.

[April 10, 1865?]
Let Master Tad have a Navy sword.[51]

1865 telegram from President Lincoln to General Ulysses Grant, sent a month before Lincoln's second inaugural, and two months prior to his April 7 telegram urging Grant to "Let the thing be pressed" (above). General Robert E. Lee surrendered to Grant at Appomattox Court House two days later.

Card of Admission for George Ashmun

The last official communication by Lincoln, issued around 8 P.M. shortly before he left the White House for Ford's Theatre.

Allow Mr. Ashmun & friend to come in at 9. A.M. to-morrow.
April 14, 1865.

The last formal photograph of Abraham Lincoln, taken by Alexander Gardner on February 5, 1865.

NOTES

Prologue

1. H. G. Wells, "The Six Greatest Men in History," *The American Magazine* (July 1922): 148, as excerpted in Harold Holzer, ed., *The Lincoln Anthology: Great Writers on His Life and Legacy from 1860 to Now* (New York: The Library of America, 2009), p. 439.

2. Ralph Waldo Emerson. "Abraham Lincoln: Remarks at the Funeral Services Held in Concord, April 19, 1865," in *The Complete Works of Ralph Waldo Emerson* (New York: W.H. Wise, 1926), as reproduced in David S. Reynolds, editor. *Lincoln's Selected Writings* (New York: Norton, 2015), pp. 422–425.

3. Karl Marx, "On Events in North America," Address of the International Working Men's Association to President Johnson, in *The Karl Marx Library, vol. II: On America and the Civil War*, edited and translated by Saul K. Padover (New York: McGraw-Hill Book Company, 1972), pp. 220–223, 241–242. Originally published in *Die Presse* (Vienna), October 12, 1862, and *The Bee-Hive* (London), May 20, 1865. Reproduced in Harold Holzer, ed., *The Lincoln Anthology*, p. 49.

4. Fred Kaplan, *Lincoln: The Biography of a Writer* (New York: HarperCollins Publishers, 2008), p. 116.

5. Jacques Barzun, *Lincoln the Writer: On Writing, Editing, and Publishing* (Chicago: University of Chicago Press, 1971), pp. 57–73, as excerpted in Harold Holzer, ed., *The Lincoln Anthology*, p. 644.

6. Kaplan, *Lincoln*, p. 21.

7. Benjamin Thomas, "Lincoln's Humor: An Analysis," *Journal of the Abraham Lincoln Association* 3, issue 1 (1981), pp. 28–47.

8. Garry Wills, *Lincoln at Gettysburg: The Words That Remade America* (New York, Simon & Schuster, 1992), p. 148.

9. Eric Foner, *The Fiery Trial: Abraham Lincoln and American Slavery* (New York: W.W. Norton, 2010), as excerpted in David S. Reynolds, ed., *Lincoln's Selected Writings* (New York: W.W. Norton, 2015), pp. 485–495.

10. Frederick Douglass, "Oration in Memory of Abraham Lincoln," April 14, 1876, Washington D.C., in *Frederick Douglass: Selected Speeches and Writings* (New York: Riverside Press, 1906), as excerpted in Reynolds, ed., *Lincoln's Selected Writings*, pp. 436–438.

Chapter 1: "Too Familiar with Disappointment to Be Much Chagrined"

1. William H. Herndon and Jesse W. Weik, *Herndon's Life of Lincoln: The History and Personal Recollections of Abraham Lincoln* (New York: Albert & Charles Boni, 1930), p. 304.

2. *Collected Works of Abraham Lincoln*, vol. 1. (Ann Arbor: University of Michigan Digital Library Production Services, 2001), p. 1, http://name.umdl.umich.edu/lincoln1.

3. Ibid., p. 5.

4. Arthur Brooks Lapsley, ed., *The Papers and Writings of Abraham Lincoln*, vol. 1, Constitutional Edition (New York: P. F. Collier and Son, 1905), http://www.gutenberg.org/files/2653/2653-h/2653-h.htm.

5. Ibid.

6. Ibid.

7. Ibid.

8. Ibid.

9. *Collected Works of Abraham Lincoln*, vol. 1, p. 229, http://name.umdl.umich.edu/lincoln1.

10. Lapsley, ed., *Papers and Writings of Abraham Lincoln*, http://www.gutenberg.org/files/2653/2653-h/2653-h.htm#link2H_4_0014.

11. Ibid.

12. *Collected Works of Abraham Lincoln*, vol. 1, p. 367, http://name.umdl.umich.edu/lincoln1.

13. Ibid.

14. Ibid.

15. Lapsley, ed., *Papers and Writings of Abraham Lincoln*, vol. 1, http://www.gutenberg.org/files/2654/2654-h/2654-h.htm#link2H_4_0019.

16. Ibid., http://www.gutenberg.org/files/2653/2653-h/2653-h.htm#link2H_4_0054.

17. *Collected Works of Abraham Lincoln*, vol. 1, p. 465, http://name.umdl.umich.edu/lincoln2.

18. Ibid., p. 477. http://name.umdl.umich.edu/lincoln1.

19. Ibid., vol. 2, p. 15, http://name.umdl.umich.edu/lincoln2.

20. Lapsley, ed., *Papers and Writings of Abraham Lincoln*, http://www.gutenberg.org/files/2654/2654-h/2654-h.htm#link2H_4_0019.

21. *Collected Works of Abraham Lincoln*, vol. 2, p. 61, http://name.umdl.umich.edu/lincoln2.

22. Ibid., p. 81, http://name.umdl.umich.edu/lincoln2.

23. Ibid., p. 96.

24. Ibid., p. 106.

Chapter 2: "As Opposite as God and Mammon"

1. *Collected Works of Abraham Lincoln*, vol. 3 (Ann Arbor: University of Michigan Digital Library, 2001), p. 386, http://name.umdl.umich.edu/lincoln3.

2. Arthur Brooks Lapsley, ed., *The Papers and Writings of Abraham Lincoln*, vol. 2, Constitutional Edition (New York: P. F. Collier and Son, 1905), http://www.gutenberg.org/files/2654/2654-h/2654-h.htm#link2H_4_0019.

3. *Collected Works of Abraham Lincoln*, vol. 2, p. 220, http://name.umdl.umich.edu/lincoln2.

4. Lapsley, ed., *Papers and Writings of Abraham Lincoln*, http://www.gutenberg.org/files/2654/2654-h/2654-h.htm#link2H_4_0019.

5. Ibid.

6. Ibid.

7. *Collected Works of Abraham Lincoln*, vol. 2, p. 362, http://name.umdl.umich.edu/lincoln2.

8. Lapsley, ed., *Papers and Writings of Abraham Lincoln*, vol. 2, http://www.gutenberg. org/files/2654/2654-h/2654-h.htm#link2H_4_0019.

9. Ibid.

10. *Collected Works of Abraham Lincoln*, vol. 2, p. 452, http://name.umdl.umich.edu/ lincoln2.

11. Lapsley, ed., *Papers and Writings of Abraham Lincoln*, vol. 2, http://www.gutenberg. org/files/2654/2654-h/2654-h.htm#link2H_4_0019.

12. *Collected Works of Abraham Lincoln*, vol. 2, p. 222, http://name.umdl.umich.edu/ lincoln2.

13. Ibid., p. 528.

14. Lapsley, ed., *Papers and Writings of Abraham Lincoln*, vol. 3, http://www.gutenberg. org/files/2655/2655-h/2655-h.htm#link2H_4_0002.

15. Ibid.

16. *Collected Works of Abraham Lincoln*, vol. 3, pp. 203, http://name.umdl.umich.edu/ lincoln3.

17. Ibid., p. 207.

18. Ibid., p. 283.

19. Lapsley, ed., *Papers and Writings of Abraham Lincoln*, vol. 3, http://www.gutenberg. org/files/2657/2657-h/2657-h.htm#link2H_4_0013.

20. *Collected Works of Abraham Lincoln*, vol. 3, p. 383, http://name.umdl.umich.edu/ lincoln3.

21. Ibid., p. 399.

22. Ibid., p. 504.

23. Lapsley, ed., *Papers and Writings of Abraham Lincoln,* vol. 5, http://www.gutenberg.org/files/2657/2657-h/2657-h.htm#link2H_4_0040.

24. Ibid., vol. 5, http://www.gutenberg.org/files/2657/2657-h/2657-h.htm#link2H_4_0013.

25. *Collected Works of Abraham Lincoln*, vol. 3, pp. 522–550, http://name.umdl.umich. edu/lincoln3.

26. Ibid., vol. 4, p. 1, http://name.umdl.umich.edu/lincoln4.

27. Ibid., p. 39.

28. Ibid., p. 45, http://quod.lib.umich.edu/l/lincoln/lincoln4/1:33?rgn=div1;view=fulltext.

29. Lapsley, ed., *Papers and Writings of Abraham Lincoln*, vol. 4, http://www.gutenberg.org/files/2657/2657-h/2657-h.htm#link2H_4_0051.

30. Ibid.

31. Ibid.

32. Ibid.

33. *Collected Works of Abraham Lincoln*, vol. 4, p. 149, http://name.umdl.umich.edu/lincoln4.

34. Ibid., p. 151.

35. Ibid., p. 160.

36. Ibid., p. 189.

37. Ibid., p. 190.

38. Ibid., p. 195.

39. Ibid., p. 236.

Chapter 3: "Without Guile, and with Pure Purpose"

1. *Collected Works of Abraham Lincoln*, vol. 4 (Ann Arbor: University of Michigan Digital Library, 2001), p. 262, http://name.umdl.umich.edu/lincoln4.

2. Ibid., p. 317.

3. Ibid., p. 322.

4. Ibid., p. 332.

5. Ibid., p. 385.

6. Ibid., p. 421.

7. Ibid., p. 482.

8. Ibid., p. 506.

9. Ibid., p. 531.

10. Ibid., p. 545.

11. Ibid., vol. 5, p. 32, http://name.umdl.umich.edu/lincoln5.

12. Ibid., p. 35.

13. Ibid., p. 222.

14. Ibid., p. 57.

15. Ibid., p. 84.

16. Ibid., p. 255.

17. Ibid., p. 268.

18. Ibid., p. 273.

19. Ibid., p. 338.

20. Ibid., p. 342.

21. Ibid., p. 370.

22. Ibid., p. 388.

Chapter 4: "Thenceforward, and Forever Free"

1. *Collected Works of Abraham Lincoln*, vol. 5 (Ann Arbor: University of Michigan Digital Library), p. 403, http://name.umdl.umich.edu/lincoln5.

2. Ibid., p. 433.

3. Ibid., p. 436.

4. Ibid., p. 436.

5. Ibid., p. 460.

6. Ibid., p. 474.

7. Ibid., p. 518 ff.

8. Ibid., vol. 6, p. 6, http://name.umdl.umich.edu/lincoln6.

9. Ibid., p. 16.

10. Ibid., p. 28.

11. Ibid., p. 63.

12. Ibid., p. 78.

13. Ibid., p. 149.

14. Ibid., p. 255.

15. Ibid., p. 260.

16. Ibid., p. 326.

17. Ibid., p. 327.

18. *The Collected Works of Abraham Lincoln: Supplement, 1832–1865* (Westport, CT: Greenwood Press, 1974), p. 194.

19. *Collected Works of Abraham Lincoln*, vol. 6, p. 371, http://name.umdl.umich.edu/lincoln6.

20. Ibid., p. 357.

21. Ibid., p. 406.

22. Ibid., p. 428.

23. Ibid., p. 474.

24. Ibid., p. 558.

25. Ibid., vol. 7, p. 17, http://name.umdl.umich.edu/lincoln7.

26. Ibid., p. 24.

27. Ibid., p. 212.

28. Ibid., p. 243.

29. Ibid., p. 281.

30. Ibid., p. 287.

31. Ibid., p. 301.

32. Ibid., p. 393.

33. Ibid., p. 406.

34. Ibid., p. 439.

35. Ibid., p. 499.

36. Ibid., p. 504.

37. Ibid., p. 514.

38. Ibid., p. 535.

39. Ibid., vol. 8, p. 116, http://name.umdl.umich.edu/lincoln8.

40. Ibid., p. 195.

41. Ibid., p. 223.

42. Ibid., p. 239.

43. Ibid., p. 266.

44. Ibid., p. 332.

45. Ibid., p. 356.

46. Ibid., p. 361.

47. Ibid., p. 381.

48. Ibid., p. 385.

49. Ibid., p. 386.

50. Ibid., p. 392.

51. Ibid., p. 395.

SUGGESTED READING

Anthologies of Writing by and about Lincoln

Fehrenbacher, Don E. (Editor). *Lincoln: Speeches and Writings 1832–1858* (New York: Library of America, 1989).

Fehrenbacher, Don E. (Editor). *Lincoln: Speeches and Writings 1859–1865* (New York: Library of America, 1989).

Holzer, Harold. *The Lincoln Anthology: Great Writers on His Life and Legacy from 1860 Until Now* (New York: Library of America, 2008).

Holzer, Harold, and Joshua Wolf Shenk (Editors). *In Lincoln's Hand: His Original Manuscripts* (New York: Bantam Dell, 2009).

Reynolds, David S. (Editor). *Lincoln's Selected Writings* (New York: W. W. Norton, 2015).

Biographies of Lincoln

Donald, David Herbert. *Lincoln* (New York: Simon & Schuster, 1995).

Goodwin, Doris Kearns. *Team of Rivals: The Political Genius of Abraham Lincoln* (New York: Simon & Schuster, 2005).

White, Ronald C., Jr. *A. Lincoln* (New York: Random House, 2009).

Lincoln as a Writer and Orator

Kaplan, Fred. *Lincoln: The Biography of a Writer* (New York: HarperCollins, 2008).

Wills, Garry. *Lincoln at Gettysburg: The Words that Remade America* (New York: Simon & Schuster, 1992).

Wilson, Douglas L. *Lincoln's Sword: The Presidency and the Power of Words* (New York: Alfred A. Knopf, 2006).

Lincoln and Slavery

Foner, Eric. *The Fiery Trial: Abraham Lincoln and American Slavery* (New York: W. W. Norton, 2010).

Books for Kids

Demi. *President Lincoln: From Log Cabin to White House* (Bloomington, IN: Wisdom Tales, 2016). Ages 7–10.

Pascal, Janet B. *Who Was Abraham Lincoln?* (New York: Grosset & Dunlap, 2008). Ages 7–10.

Freedman, Russell. *Abraham Lincoln and Frederick Douglass: The Story Behind an American Friendship* (New York: Houghton Mifflin Harcourt, 2012). Ages 9–14.

Videos

Kunhardt Productions. *Abraham Lincoln: The Making of a President* (1992). Four parts.

INDEX

Photographs, illustrations, and artwork
are indicated with **bold**.

PHOTO CREDITS

Abraham Lincoln Presidential Library & Museum (ALPLM), 18, 186

Courtesy McLellan Lincoln Collection, John Hay Library, Brown University, 150, 177

Courtesy of Seth Kaller Inc., www.sethkaller.com, 9

Division of Rare and Manuscript Collections, Cornell University Library, 187

The Gilder Lehrman Institute, 62

Library of Congress, ii, vi, 1, 2, 3, 6, 12, 14, 23, 31, 32, 35, 43, 44, 45, 49, 52, 57, 59, 70, 71, 77, 84, 89, 91, 93, 94, 95, 97, 101, 102, 103, 105, 110, 111, 113, 116, 120, 103, 133, 141, 143, 146–147, 148, 155, 158, 164, 170, 171, 175, 179, 183, 184, 185, 189, 198, 200, 203, 204, 205, 206, 210

National Archives, 4, 212

New York State Library, 152

Quincy Public Library, 73

Shapell Manuscript Foundation, 126

William E. Barton Collection of Lincolniana, Special Collections Research Center, University of Chicago Library, 7, 8

All other images are in the public domain.